# HAPPY NOWRUZ

Cooking with Children to Celebrate
the Persian New Year

## Najmieh Batmanglij

MAGE PUBLISHERS
WASHINGTON, DC

## A NOTE FROM THE AUTHOR AND PUBLISHER

Keep in mind: Children should not use this book without adult supervision. The author and publisher have tried their best to express the importance of safety when children are cooking in the kitchen. Neither the author nor publisher can assume responsibility for any accidents, injuries, losses, or other damages resulting from the use of this book.

**LIBRARY OF CONGRESS CATALOGING-IN-PUBLICATION DATA**
Batmanglij, Najmieh,
Happy Nowruz : cooking with children to celebrate the Persian New Year /
Najmieh Batmanglij. -- 1st hardcover ed.
p. cm.
ISBN 1-933823-16-X (hardcover : alk. paper)
1. Cookery, Iranian--Juvenile literature. 2. Nawruz (Festival)--Juvenile literature.
3. Food habits--Iran--Juvenile literature. I. Title.
TX725.I7B367 2008
641.5955--dc22
2007036047

First Print on Demand Edition
ISBN: 1-933823-71-2
ISBN-13: 978-1933823-71-3

PRINTED IN USA

MAGE PUBLISHERS
202-342-1642 • AS@MAGE.COM
VISIT MAGE ONLINE AT
WWW.MAGE.COM

For children everywhere,
and for their parents,
Happy Nowruz!

# Contents

# Preface

**Living in America, my family and I welcome every holiday** and joyful occasion, and we get more pleasure than ever from celebrating Nowruz – the Persian New Year.

Through the years I have found myself going out of my way to be more creative and inventive when celebrating the traditional New Year ceremonies with my children outside of Iran. Nowruz is a spiritual holiday, not a religious one – it is a celebration of the arrival of spring and the rebirth of nature. Everyone can enjoy Nowruz, no matter where they live.

In writing this book, I was inspired by my childhood experiences of Nowruz in Iran in the 1950s and 1960s, as well as by more than twenty-five years of celebrating Nowruz with my own children outside of Iran. I hope that families and children everywhere can benefit from our experience.

This book is suitable for all ages and can be used at various levels – parents and teachers could read it out loud to children under seven years of age, while older children can do everything in the book, including preparing the various dishes and cookies with the help of parents or teachers. Ideally, I would like to inspire the whole family to get together and have fun with the various activities involved in preparing for the arrival of spring and the rebirth of nature. It can be a joyful experience for everyone in the family to cook their favorite foods together. I have created simple recipes so that children as well as adults who don't normally cook can participate in the preparation of the meal. Most of the recipes in this book are traditionally made during the Nowruz holidays, but I have also added a few of my and my children's favorites, such as making flatbreads and topping them to make a wonderful pizza. I hope you will enjoy reading this book and cooking from it as much as I have enjoyed working on it.

# An Ancient Tradition

**Joyful and filled with feasting,** Nowruz – or "new day" – is Iran's happiest family holiday. It comes on the first day of spring, on the vernal equinox – March 20, 21, or 22 – when the sun crosses the celestial equator. Day and night are the same length, spring greenery and flowers start to adorn trees and fields, and the Iranian year begins. But as we'll see, preparations for the festivities start several weeks earlier, and the celebrations continue for a full thirteen days.

The festival and its customs have roots as long and tangled as the noodles in a traditional Nowruz soup. Some trace the New Year customs back 5,000 years to the spring festivals of Sumer and Babylon, with their dying and reborn gods. Others refer to King Jamshid, whose first celebration of Nowruz is recounted in Ferdowsi's *Shahnameh.* Still others point to the prophet Zoroaster and the Persian empire.

Certainly, the New Year was celebrated each spring at Persepolis 2,500 years ago, when ambassadors from around the great Persian empire would bring fabulous gifts. Even today in the ruins of that mighty palace you can see their images on the staircases leading to the audience hall of Darius the Great. Up those stairs the carvings march, Scythians and Cilicians with rams, Bactrians with camels, Ionians with yarns.

As we'll see, many different strands are interwoven through Nowruz. It is not a religious holiday, but it has echoes of ancient mythologies and little-known legends.

Many people from different parts of the world celebrate Nowruz. From Iraq to Afghanistan to parts of China, Tajiks, Chinese, Indians, Kurds, and Azerbaijanis all take part. For many Iranians living in countries around the world, this spring festival is a time to come together and celebrate.

# Celebrate Spring

**Nowruz is a time for cleansing and renewal** – of the house, of the spirit, of family ties and friendships. It celebrates light, fire, water, and the rebirth of nature after the winter. It is a time of rejoicing, visiting, partying, and gift giving. And, like any happy family holiday, it features time-honored customs and cooking.

In the pages that follow, we'll explore Nowruz in all its pleasant aspects. We'll introduce Haji Firuz, the herald who brings word of the New Year, and show how Iranians prepare for the festival. We'll describe the celebrations. We'll explain how to set a traditional New Year's table and why each item on it appears. We'll look at the customs and feasting of the day itself and of the days that follow. And finally, we'll offer a collection of my favorite Nowruz recipes so that parents and children, as well as teachers and their students, can cook together to celebrate the arrival of spring.

At the end of the book, there is a brief look at the Iranian calendar, which measures the turning year. This will help readers to see how Nowruz happens and find its ancient roots.

# The Arrival of Haji Firuz

**In Iran, the first sign** that Nowruz is near is the appearance of dancers and singers – called Haji Firuz – in every neighborhood disguised with masks, animal skins, and makeup, with some wearing tall, red hats. Through the streets they dance, playing tambourines, trumpets, and drums, and singing to passersby. The first performers appear about two weeks before Nowruz. As the day draws nearer, more and more of these heralds are seen, dancing for the joys of the holiday.

How did this charming custom come to be? Some believe Haji Firuz is a relic of Tammuz, the long-forgotten Sumerian god of sacrifice, who was said to die at the end of each winter and to be reborn each spring; Haji Firuz's darkened face is a sign of his return from the underworld, the red clothing a symbol of the blood sacrifice.

No one really knows where Haji Firuz originated. Most believe, though, that his red costume and his hat – which looks like a rising flame – recall the sacred fire of Ahura Mazda, the Zoroastrian Lord of Wisdom. In this way, Haji Firuz stands for the victory of light over darkness, good over evil, and spring over winter.

The children who follow the dancer through the streets don't care about his origins. They just like to listen to the simple songs he sings.

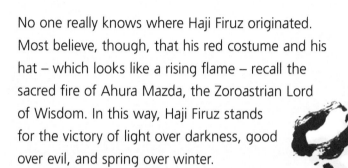

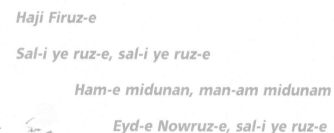

*Haji Firuz-e*

*Sal-i ye ruz-e, sal-i ye ruz-e*

*Ham-e midunan, man-am midunam*

*Eyd-e Nowruz-e, sal-i ye ruz-e*

**Haji Firuz is here**

**It's once a year, it's once a year**

**Everyone knows it's here, I know it's here**

**Nowruz is here, it comes but once a year**

# Preparing for Nowruz

**Once Haji Firuz appears,** Iranian households buzz with activity. Nowruz is a time of beginnings, and everything must be bright, fresh, and new.

For parents, these two weeks are a time to clean the house from top to bottom – dusting, washing, and polishing until everything shines – readying it for spring by throwing out the old and bringing in the new.

**This is also a good time for families to:**

- Buy new clothes

- Get haircuts

- Pay debts and return anything borrowed

- Catch up on homework or chores

**Nowruz is also a time for cleaning the spirit. It is a time to:**

- Forgive oneself and others for wrongdoings

- Settle disagreements

- Apologize for any bad behavior in the past year

- Ask for explanations from anyone who has hurt you

- Talk over any problems or concerns with adults and parents

# Activities to Welcome Nowruz

There are many things that adults and children can do together to welcome the holiday season. These are some of the activities that my children enjoyed:

- Germinating seeds for sprouts

- Planting narcissus and hyacinth bulbs in pots

- Selecting, buying, and taking care of goldfish

- Dyeing and decorating eggs (see page 25)

- Painting banners and balloons with Nowruz resolutions such as "good words, good thoughts, good deeds," for decorating the house and classroom

- Making holiday cards that say, "Happy Nowruz" or, in Persian, *"Eyd-e Shoma Mobarak"* or *"Nowruz-e tan piruz,"* for sending to friends and family

- Making Nowruz cookies, especially Haji Firuz gingerbread cookies

- Making garlands hung with flowers, fruits, photos, favorite stickers, and Haji Firuz gingerbread cookies

# Preparing Sprouts

To make sprouts, you can use various grains such as wheat, mung beans, or lentils, and the resulting sprouts look different. The sprouts on these two pages are lentil sprouts; those on page 38 are wheat sprouts. I prefer sprouts from lentils, but you can experiment and see which ones you like best.

- Put 1 cup of dried lentils in a bowl, cover with cold water, and soak for 2 days or more, changing the water once a day. Tiny white tendrils will appear, showing that the lentils are germinating.

- Drain the lentils and transfer to a cotton dish towel. Tie it up loosely and place it back in the bowl. Spray it with water twice a day for 2 to 3 days or more until little green/white sprouts appear on the lentils.

- Once the little green/white sprouts have appeared, remove the sprouted lentils from the dish towel and spread them evenly in an 8-inch-diameter flat dish (you can also place about 1 tablespoon's worth in the eggshells shown on the pages that follow).

- Cover the dish with the dish towel, spray the towel with water to moisten twice a day for 2 to 3 days until the sprouts are about a half inch tall.

- Uncover the sprouts, place in a sunny room, and continue to keep moist by spraying once a day.

# Eggshell Sprouts

## To Prepare Eggshells

If you would like to decorate your eggshells with dye, you will need to do that first (see pages 25–27).

For this project you'll need some germinated seeds (see page 21), a cotton dish towel, a sprayer or mister, and a dozen eggs.

- With adult help, use a sharp knife to slice off the narrow ends of 12 eggs. Empty the contents into an airtight jar and refrigerate for another use (to make Fresh herb kuku on page 63, perhaps).

- Rinse the eggshells with cold water and put them back in their carton.

- Put 1 tablespoon of germinated lentil grains into each eggshell. Place the egg carton in a sunny spot and cover with the dish towel.

- Spray the dish towel with water twice a day for 2 to 3 days. Don't soak the sprouts: they'll rot. But don't allow them to dry out.

- Once the lentils have sprouted green/white, remove the cloth. Spray with water twice a day, and in several days you'll have wonderful eggshell sprouts.

## Tips, Tools, & Ingredients

● Use a work surface that's a comfortable height – a low table that comes up to the waist is ideal. If you don't have one, children can stand on a footstool at the kitchen counter. Cover the surface with several layers of paper towels to catch spills.

● A frame in which the dyed eggs can dry. An egg carton is perfect. Snip off the bottom of each egg cup with scissors or punch it out with your fingers. The hollow rings you create will hold drying eggs upright.

● A saucepan for boiling eggs and tongs for moving them around

● Disposable latex gloves

● An 8-ounce bowl for each color you use

● A long cooking needle

● Hard-boiled cooked or hollowed-out eggs (white eggs show certain colors better)

● Natural food coloring (sold in the cake-decorating sections of most supermarkets)

● White vinegar

Remember that raw eggs must never be eaten. They may harbor salmonella. Hard-boiled eggs should be stored in the refrigerator until it's time to decorate the Nowruz table.

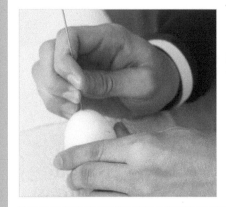

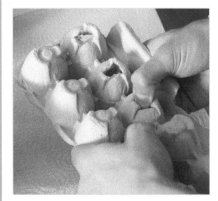

# Egg Decorating

Since the first farmers saw newborn chicks and ducklings emerging from their shells, the egg has been one of the great symbols of fertility and rebirth. In fact, many early creation myths – those of India, Egypt, and Greece, for instance – depicted the universe as emerging from a vast cosmic egg that floated in space or in primeval waters. It's not surprising, then, that eggs are part of the rites of spring all over the world.

Eggs have been an important part of Iran's Nowruz festivities for thousands of years. Every Nowruz table displays colored eggs. Alone or in groups of three or seven, eggs rest on a mirror as a symbol of fertility. Decorated eggs can adorn Nowruz garlands, and eggshells may serve as miniature pots for germinating sprouts – those symbols of renewal that adorn the Nowruz table (see page 36) and the Outdoor Thirteen picnic (see page 53).

Creating these pretty eggs at home is a happy Nowruz custom. Parents, teachers, and children can color hard-boiled eggs or eggshells with food dyes – or with traditional dyes, using onion skins, beets, saffron, and turmeric – that have been used for centuries.

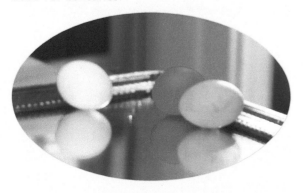

## Hollowing Out Eggshells

- Wash and dry uncooked eggs.
- Use a long cooking needle to make a small hole in the larger end of each egg, twisting the needle in as far as you can.
- Make a larger hole in the smaller end of each egg, using the needle as shown on the facing page.
- Move the needle around inside the shell to break the yolk.
- Hold the egg over a bowl, place your lips over the larger hole, and blow until all the egg comes out of the smaller hole. (Refrigerate the egg contents for use in Fresh Herb Kuku.)
- Gently run water into the egg to rinse it out. Blow out the water, and set the egg in your egg holder to dry. It is now ready for dyeing with food coloring.

## Boiling Eggs

- Place 4 white eggs in a medium saucepan and cover with cold water.
- Set the saucepan over medium heat and bring the water to a boil.
- Use oven mitts to remove the pan from the heat, cover, and allow to rest for 10 minutes.
- Using tongs, transfer the eggs to the egg frame and cool before dyeing.

## Using Food Coloring

● On your work surface, set out one 8-ounce bowl for each color you are going to use.

● Add 1 cup of hot water and 3 tablespoons of white vinegar to each bowl. Then stir in 10 drops of food coloring, using one color per bowl.

● Using disposable gloves or tongs, set one egg at a time in one of the colored liquids. Let it rest a few moments. Transfer the egg to the egg frame and let dry completely before refrigerating.

# Coloring Eggs

## Using Ancient Dyes

For this project you'll need to ask for adult help and use oven mitts when handling hot saucepans. You will also need uncooked white eggs, 4 red onions, and ground turmeric.

## Red Eggs

- Peel the skins and outer layers from the 4 red onions.
- Place the onion layers between 4 white eggs in a small saucepan. Add 2 cups of water and 3 tablespoons of white vinegar.
- Set the pan over medium heat and bring the water to a boil. Then cover the pan, reduce the heat to low, and simmer for 8 minutes.
- Remove the pan from the heat and allow the eggs to cool in the water. Once they've cooled, transfer them to your egg holder.

## Yellow Eggs

- Follow the onion dyeing instructions above, using 2 tablespoons of ground turmeric instead of onion skins.

A 30-foot length of
floral wire; fairy lights
and a glue gun; 7 dyed,
hollowed-out eggs; as
many Nowruz symbols
listed below as you can
collect:

- pomegranates
- apples
- oranges
- orange leaves
- grapes
- figs
- olive branches
- hyacinths
- narcissi
- small mirrors
- small, framed family
  pictures
- gold coins
- Nowruz greeting cards
- artificial goldfish
- Haji Firuz Ginger-
  bread Cookies

# A Nowruz Garland

Some years ago, when celebrating Nowruz in America,
I made a garland of colorful Nowruz symbols. Since
then, we have prepared one every year – it's fun to do,
festive and very decorative.

- With adult help, measure the length of the area
  where the garland will be suspended and cut the
  wire with an extra 12 inches on either side. Lay
  the wire on a work surface or on the floor and use
  a glue gun or small pieces of wire to attach the
  eggs to the wire at 10-inch intervals.

- In between the eggs attach as many Nowruz
  symbols as you like. Choose among pomegranates;
  apples; oranges; orange leaves; grapes; figs; olive
  branches; hyacinths; narcissi; small mirrors; small,
  framed family pictures; gold coins; Nowruz greeting
  cards; artificial goldfish; Haji Firuz Gingerbread
  Cookies; and most importantly – for light is a
  symbol of Nowruz – small lightbulbs
  (fairy lights).

- Suspend the garland over your Nowruz table or
  drape it over a mantel or stair rail.

# Wild Fire Eve
## CHAHAR SHANBEH SURI

**Transitions between seasons** are "open" times in folklore, times when spirits slip into the world and ghosts walk among the living.

In Iranian folklore, there is a character called Amu Nowruz (Uncle Nowruz) who personifies the visits of ancestors during Nowruz, and who leaves signs of his visits in the form of gifts or flowers. In ancient Iran (and in Iran and India today), Zoroastrians held a Suri – red or fiery – festival to welcome New Year's spirits. In the days preceding the equinox, clay figurines of departed relatives and animals were placed on rooftops to welcome back the spirits. As well, bonfires were lit during the nights to give the spirits the light of sacred fire and protect them from evil, as well as to illuminate their paths home.

These almost-forgotten customs are echoed in Iran on the last Tuesday night before Nowruz – Wild Fire Eve. All of this activity was once meant to frighten evil spirits so that the last Wednesday of the old year would be calm. Now Wild Fire Eve Festival is just for fun – much like Halloween in America. Children begin the celebrations early in the evening with spoon banging and going door to door trick-or-treating; later on there's fireworks and the Bonfire Festival. The entertainment winds up with a feast of Nowruz soup, nuts, and sweets.

# The Banging of Spoons
## GASHOGH-ZANI

**Dressed as ghosts in sheets** or chadors (shrouds), Iranian children troop through the twilight streets of their neighborhoods with friends making a terrific racket by banging pots with spoons and asking for treats from their neighbors. All of the noise and commotion – including fireworks throughout the town – is supposed to frighten away any lurking evil spirits, making room for the guardian angels of the new year.

When darkness falls, bonfires begin to shine in private gardens, and in public streets and alleys. Families (adults should always be present when making fires) dance around them, leaping over the flames and shouting:

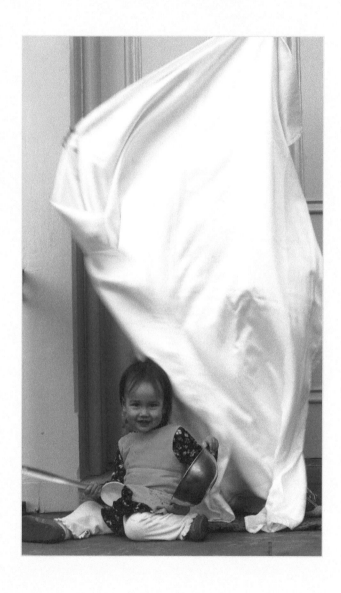

*Sorkhi-e to az man o zardi-e man az to!*
Give me your beautiful red color
        and take back my sickly pallor!

This ritual is a way of burying the mistakes and problems of the old year and preparing to shine in the new.

# Feasting and Fun
## AJIL-E CHAHAR SHANBEH SURI AND ASH-E RESHTEH

**Wild Fire Eve is a night** when wishes come true, a night when Iranians prepare special dishes to give to family, friends, and strangers – especially needy strangers – who return a blessing and a prayer. In our house, we gather around a large tray of nuts and dried fruit. We shell the nuts, and bless the food by chanting and praying. The combination of fruits and nuts, called *Ajil-e Chahar Shanbeh Suri,* is composed of seven ingredients, which often include: **pistachios, roasted chickpeas, almonds, hazelnuts, figs, apricots,** and **raisins.**

Even more warming is the *Ash-e Reshteh,* the Nowruz noodle and bean soup that has been simmering away all day. Legend says that if you make a wish while helping with the soup, the wish will come true. Is it any wonder that everyone helps with the preparations?

- **Sabzeh**    Sprouts
- **Sib**    Apples
- **Sonbol**    Hyacinth
- **Serkeh**    Wine Vinegar
- **Seer**    Garlic
- **Senjed**    Wild Olives
- **Somaq**    Sumac

# Nowruz Holiday Table
## SOFREH-YE HAFT-SINN

**Perhaps the most beautiful Nowruz** tradition is the holiday table arranged in every Iranian household in time to greet the New Year. The essential elements are placed on a special cloth, called *sofreh,* that is spread on a carpet or table, and when arrangements are complete, the setting is rich in the symbols of Iranian mythology and belief. It becomes a story of fertility and renewal, just as each New Year recalls the original creation.

Central to the setting is the number seven, echoing the belief in the mystic power that people have attributed to that number since civilization began. To the ancients, everything that mattered was grouped in sevens. For instance, they recognized seven "planets": the sun, the moon, Mercury, Venus, Mars, Jupiter, and Saturn. The planets influenced the seven senses – sight, hearing, taste, smell, touch, heat and cold, body awareness – that shaped the human spirit. At the peak of the Zoroastrian pantheon, led by Ahura Mazda, the Lord of Wisdom, were the Seven Immortals who guarded all of creation: sky, waters, earth, fire, plants, animals, and humans.

In ancient Persia, people celebrated Nowruz by growing seven kinds of seeds on seven pillars *(sutuns).* If the seeds prospered, so would the crops in the coming year. These men and women decorated their Nowruz tables with trays bearing seven branches – of wheat, barley, peas, rice, pomegranate, olive, almond, and fig – and they made a ceremonial Nowruz loaf from seven kinds of grain.

In addition to the number seven, the letter "s" is also central to the Nowruz table. According to legend, the first Nowruz was signaled by the sudden appearance of seven *sabzeh,* or greens (green is the color associated with Nowruz), each of which began with the letter "s," or sinn in Persian. Each item on the Nowruz table also recalls qualities of the Seven Immortals, who herald renewal and rebirth – the source of the joy of Nowruz. The items are listed on the facing page with details on the pages that follow.

Sabzeh · Sprouts
RENEWAL

# Seven Items
## HAFT-SINN

SIB
**Apples**
FERTILITY & BEAUTY

SONBOL
**Hyacinth**
FRAGRANCE

SERKEH
**Wine Vinegar**
IMMORTALITY & ETERNITY

SEER
**Garlic**
HEALTH & FERTILITY

SENJED
**Wild Olives**
FERTILITY & LOVE

SOMAQ
**Sumac**
FERTILITY

Eggs
FERTILITY

# Other Elements of the Nowruz Table
RU-YE SOFREH-YE HAFT-SINN

A brazier for burning wild rue, a sacred herb that was thought to ward off evil spirits.

A mirror to reflect the light of the Lord of Wisdom and the images of his creation.

A book of the poetry of Hafez, and/or a copy of the Holy Qur'an.

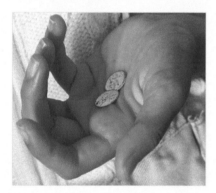

A few coins for bounty.

A flask of rose water for its cleansing power and sweet fragrance.

An orange floating in a bowl of water, representing the earth as it floats in space.

A goldfish in a bowl of water for: the beginning of creation: Khordad, the immortal who guarded the waters, and Anahita, the goddess of water.

Samanu, wheat sprout pudding, is called magic pudding. Without adding sugar, the flour and sprouts become sweet when cooked.

Lit candles for holy fire.

# Gathering to Welcome Nowruz
## PISHVAZ-E TAHVIL-E SAL

**A few hours before** the New Year begins, Iranian families gather with friends around the decorated Nowruz table, the *sofreh-ye haft-sinn*. This is the hour for making wishes and for a beloved Iranian pastime: exploring the *ghazals* – poems – of the great fourteenth-century Persian poet Hafez for glimpses of the future.

The oldest person at the gathering who can read Hafez asks all the guests to close their eyes and make wishes. Then holding the book of Hafez poems closed, with its spine in his or her left hand, the reader strokes the edges of the pages with the right index finger and recites this supplication:

> *Ay Hafez-e Shiraz-I to ke mahram-e har raz-i*
> *To ra be Shakh-e Nabatat qassam be ma begu ke*
> *sal-e now che khahad shod*

> O Hafez of Shiraz, knower of all secrets
> By the love of your sweetheart, Shakh-e Nabat...
> Let us know what the New Year has in store for us.

Having made the formal plea, the eldest strokes down the page edges, opens the book at random, and glances at the first poem to meet the eye.

All the guests cry out, "Read the poem! Read the poem!" And the poem is read. Its sense and mood gives each person a hint as to how a wish will be granted.

# Old Signs of Spring

**When civilization was young** the bull was a sacred animal, often associated with the moon and thought to rule the rhythms of the universe. Ancient Persians believed that the axis on which the world turned was the horn of a giant bull. Once a year at the spring equinox, they said, the bull tossed his burden from one horn to the other. The exact instant of transition could be observed on the ceremonial table in the tiniest movement of the egg resting on its mirror or of the orange floating in its bowl.

# The Transit of Years
## TAHVIL-E SAL

**The exact moment of the equinox** – the instant we pass from the old year to the new – is a solemn one. This is the moment, according to tradition, when the spirits of our ancestors, or our guardian angels, actually descend to visit us. Every preparation we've made – the spring cleaning, the special foods, the decoration of the Nowruz table, and the lighting of its candles – is meant to show us at our best so as to honor the spirits and give them joy in us.

The actual moment of transition is a time for meditation and prayer. Family and friends are gathered around the shining Nowruz table. Once again the eldest leads, reciting a prayer for everyone to repeat:

> O Swayer of our heart and sight
> O Governor of day and night
> O Swayer of feeling and thought
> Bring us to that state of delight

In Iran, the moment passes with an announcement on radio or television: Nowruz has begun. The eldest stands and gives everyone sweets, coins, and lots of hugs, and children receive bank notes or gifts *(aydi)* from their elders. Now family and friends will share their New Year's feast, give presents, visit, and, on the thirteenth day after Tahvil, picnic outdoors to greet the spring.

# My Nowruz Menu

**In the days just before Nowruz –** and on the day itself – the entire family gathers to prepare the feast that they will share after the transition to the New Year. They also make sweets to serve family and friends during holiday visits.

### Flatbread
Nan

### Flatbread Pizza
Pideh

### Cheese, Fresh Herb, Fruit, and Nut Sandwich
Nan-o panir-o sabzi khordan

### Noodle Soup
Ash-e reshteh

### Red Rice with Green Beans
Lubia polow

### Fresh Herb Kuku with Barberries
Kuku-ye zabzi ba zereshk

### Yogurt and Cucumber Dip
Mast-o khiar

### Green Rice
Sabzi polow

### Fish Strips
Mahi-e tanuri

# Nowruz Sweets

**These are my favorite Nowruz sweets,** which I have cooked with my children when they were small. We had fun in making up names for them in English.

**Haji Firuz Gingerbread Cookies**
Nun-e ghandi

**Nowruz Cupcakes**
Keyk-e yazdi

**Cream Puff**
Nun-e khameyi

**Cinnamon Date Bun**
Kolucheh

**Chewy Raisin Cookies**
Nun-e keshmeshi

**Walnut Kiss Cookies**
Nun-e gerdui

**Almond Candy Cookies**
Nun-e badami

**Rice Cookies**
Nun-e berenji

**Sweet Almond Berries**
Tut

**Four-Leaf Clover Cookies**
Nun-e nokhodchi

**Honey Almond Candy Crunch**
Sohan asaly

**Baklava**
Baqlava

**Puff Pastry Tongues**
Zaban

**Pomegranate Popsicles**
Alaska-ye anar

**Crunch Cream Ice Cream Sandwich**
Bastami-e nuni

**Sour Cherry Cooler**
Sharbat-e albalu

# A Round of New Year's Visits
## DID-O BAZ-DID

**Nowruz day is** for wishes, blessings, and feasting, but the celebrations go on for twelve more days. These are days of visitings, and they have their own traditions. The Nowruz table remains set for the season; every house is adorned with narcissi, hyacinths, and the blossoms of fruit trees. The samovar is ready with tea, and trays are piled high with sweets to offer guests.

The visits have their own protocol. For the first three days of Nowruz, the older generation remains at home to welcome the younger. Children go from house to house bearing presents – bunches of flowers or pastries – to show their respect. In return, parents and grandparents make a little ceremony of offering *aydi,* or gifts of crisp new notes of money. Sometimes they'll bless the notes by placing them in a holy book. Other times, they write a message or "Happy Nowruz" and the year on the bank notes.

After the third day, the elders repay the visits. Everyone has the chance to be both host and guest in this happy season.

# The Outdoor Thirteen Picnic
## SIZDAH BEDAR

**When the twelve** festive days of Nowruz are complete, it's time to end the holiday. The final party is always held outdoors: It's a day for picnicking and games.

This is the Outdoor Thirteen picnic in honor of Tir – the Zoroastrian angel of the rains – who gives his name to the day (but, we hope, doesn't rain on it). Iranians like to choose a grassy spot, preferably near a stream, to enjoy the spring weather.

Off they go, entire families carrying rugs to sit on and all sorts of picnic food, including kabobs, green rice, herb kuku, yogurt dip and Nowruz noodle soup. This is a day for good food – and for games. The picnickers play backgammon and chess. Youngsters play sports. There is always plenty of music, and everyone sings and dances throughout the day.

Last but not least, the family ends the holiday by throwing sprouts saved from the Nowruz table into the water of a stream or pond. By tossing the sprouts as far away from home as possible, the family throws out any evil spirits who might lurk in the house, ensuring that the coming year will be both happy and lucky.

# When Children Cook

## A WORD TO ADULTS

- Be sure that children have a work surface that is the right height for them (waist level).

- Help children to organize and prepare for making a recipe. Use a baking sheet or tray to hold measured ingredients in bowls or containers.

- Be sure that you have discussed how to work with a stove.

- In this book I have used coarse or kosher salt. If you use regular salt, reduce the amount of salt specified in the recipe because it is saltier than coarse or kosher salt.

**Be extra careful when children:**

- Place baking sheets in the hot oven and remove them;

- Lift the lid off of anything containing boiling water;

- Use serrated or pairing knives;

- Chop or slice ingredients.

## A WORD TO CHILDREN

- Be sure an adult is present whenever you work in the kitchen.

- Chopping herbs takes practice; ask an adult to help. Use a mezzaluna to make chopping much simpler.

- Read the recipes, make a list of the ingredients you need; and, if necessary, go shopping with an adult for anything not readily available in the kitchen.

- Before you start cooking gather all the ingredients for the recipe you plan to make. Measure the ingredients carefully and place them in containers on a baking sheet so that you have everything you need in one place (called *mis en place* in French, which means "everything in its place").

- Place the tools you will need for the recipe on the kitchen counter.

- Always wash your hands before cooking.

- Wear an apron.

- Always use oven mitts to move pots on the stove, lift lids, or remove baking sheets from the oven.

MAKES: 4 LOAVES
PREPARATION TIME: 25 MINUTES, AND
90 MINUTES FOR DOUGH TO RISE
COOKING TIME: 5 MINUTES PER LOAF

## ingredients

**warm water** 1 cup
(around 115°F, 45°C)

**active dry yeast** 1 package
(2 teaspoons)

**sugar** 1 teaspoon

**olive oil** 1 tablespoon

**unbleached all-purpose
flour** 2½ cups plus ½ cup
for dusting

**sea salt** 1 teaspoon

**nigella seeds** 1 tablespoon

TOPPINGS

**nigella seeds** 1 teaspoons

**sesame seeds** 1 teaspoons

**poppy seeds** 1 teaspoons

## special tools

instant-read thermometer;
rolling pin; parchment paper;
pastry brush; plastic wrap;
clean cloth for wrapping

# Flatbread

## NAN

## 1 Before you start

- Gather all the ingredients and tools and ask for adult help, especially when using the oven.

## 2 Making the dough

- In a small bowl dissolve the yeast in the warm water. Add the sugar and leave for 10 minutes undisturbed.
- Add the oil and stir well with a wooden spoon. Set aside.
- In a large shallow bowl sift 2½ cups of flour and the salt.
- Gradually stir in the dissolved yeast to the flour until you have a sticky dough. Add 1 tablespoon nigella seeds.

## 3 Let the dough rise

- Gather the dough and make a ball. Wipe the bowl and oil it with 1 tablespoon olive oil.
- Place the dough in the bowl, and turn it in the oil to coat it evenly all over.
- Cover the bowl with plastic wrap and place it in a draft-free spot in the kitchen. Allow it to rise for 1 hour (or overnight in the fridge).
- Poke the dough with your finger. If the indent stays, the dough is ready; if not, cover and allow to rise some more.

## 4 Prepare oven

- Place the oven rack in the lowest position.
- Preheat the oven to 500°F (260°C).

## 5 Shaping the dough

- Oil a baking sheet with one teaspoon of oil.
- Turn the dough out onto a lightly floured work surface and punch down. Shape the dough into an 8-inch rectangle.
- Cut the dough into 4 equal pieces and shape each piece into a ball. Place them 6 inches apart on the oiled baking sheet. Cover with plastic wrap and allow the dough to rest for 30 minutes.

baking continued on next page

## 6  Making the topping

- In a small bowl combine the sesame, nigella and poppy seeds.

## 7  Baking the flatbread "nan"

- Flatten one of the balls of dough and roll it out with a rolling pin as far as it will go. Allow it to rest for a minute then roll out some more (once the gluten has stretched it can be rolled further). Roll out until you have a thin sheet.

- Place the rolled-out dough on an oiled baking sheet. Lightly brush it with 1 teaspoon of water. Use a fork to lightly stripe the surface of the dough. Sprinkle some of the seeds over it.

- Place the baking sheet in the oven and bake for 4 to 5 minutes, until lightly brown and crispy.

- **Ask for adult help** and use oven mitts to remove the baking sheet from the oven. Repeat for the remaining *nans*.

- Make a pile of your *nans* and cover with a clean kitchen cloth, or wrap in plastic to keep soft until ready to eat.

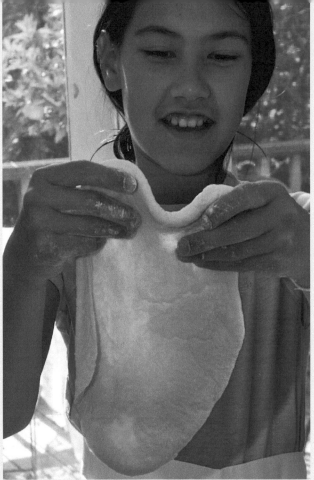

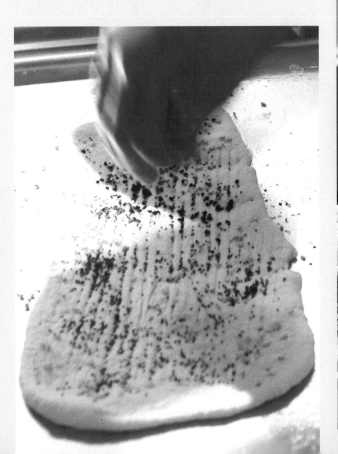

# Flatbread Pizza
## PIDEH

Flatbreads are the oldest forms of bread and probably the basis for the first pizza (when various toppings were added).

- Line a baking sheet with a piece of parchment paper or baking mat.
- Place a prepared flattened loaf on the parchment paper.
- Brush it with olive oil.
- Sprinkle with 1 teaspoon of seeds (leaving a half-inch border around the edge).
- Add 1 tablespoon of grated parmigiano reggiano cheese.
- Spread sliced fresh tomato over it.
- Sprinkle with 2 tablespoons of shredded mozzarella over the tomato.
- Drizzle some olive oil on top. Sprinkle with salt and pepper and add sprigs of fresh oregano, basil, and any other of your favorite toppings (my favorites are cheese, tomato, garlic and red pepper flakes).
- Bake for 11 to 12 minutes until the crust is brown and crisp.

# Cheese, Fresh Herb, Fruit, and Nut Sandwich
## NAN-O PANIR-O SABZI KHORDAN

### 1 Before you start, gather

- fresh aromatic herbs such as tarragon, basil, cilantro, dill, mint, radishes, and scallions;
- fresh fruits and vegetables such as grapes, cucumbers, and melons;
- nuts, including shelled walnuts, almonds, or pistachios;
- goat cheese or a Feta-type cheese;
- flatbread, pita, lavash, sangak, or barbary (I prefer the whole wheat versions that are readily available these days, for they taste better to me and they are better for your body).

### 2 Washing and preparing herbs and fruit

- Pick over the herbs and remove any wilted leaves. Snip the stems and trim the radishes and scallions.
- Place herbs in a large container of cold water, add a tablespoon of vinegar, and soak for 10 minutes. Drain, rinse thoroughly, and pat dry.
- Place the grapes in a large container of cold water and wash thoroughly. Peel and slice melons and cucumbers.

### 3 Toasting

- With adult help, toast the nuts by placing them in a long-handled skillet over medium heat. Shake the skillet constantly for a few minutes. Remove from heat and set aside to cool.
- Prepare the cheese by cutting it into small cubes or slices.
- Toast the flatbread so that it is hot but not too crisp.

### 4 Serving

- Place all ingredients on a platter or in a basket. Cover with a large, white napkin or cloth until ready to use.
- Combine a little of everything according to your taste and enjoy one of my all-time favorite sandwiches – a meal in itself or a side dish to any great meal.

MAKES: 1 BAKING SHEET OF KUKU
PREPARATION TIME: 40 MINUTES
COOKING TIME: 30 MINUTES

## ingredients

**fresh parsley** 2 cups, finely chopped

**fresh cilantro leaves** 2 cups, finely chopped

**fresh dill** 2 cups, chopped

**scallions** 2 cups, finely chopped

**eggs** 12

**baking powder** 1 teaspoon

**advieh** (Persian spice mix) 2 teaspoons

**coarse salt** 2 teaspoons

**black pepper** 1 teaspoon, freshly ground

**garlic** 4 cloves, peeled and grated

**dried fenugreek leaves** 1 tablespoon

**all-purpose flour** 2 tablespoons

**olive oil** ½ cup

DECORATION
**barberries** 1 cup
**oil** 2 tablespoons
**sugar** 2 tablespoons

## special tools

fine-mesh colander

mezzaluna for chopping herbs

parchment paper (enough to cover a baking sheet)

rubber spatula

flat metal spatula

# Fresh Herb Kuku with Barberries
## KUKU-YE ZABZI BA ZERESHK

### 1 Before you start

- Gather all the ingredients and tools. Ask for adult help, especially for cutting and chopping vegetables and herbs, and using the oven and stove top.

### 2 Preparing the herbs

- Soak the parsley, cilantro, dill, and scallions for 15 minutes in a large container of cold water. Drain and rinse three times to remove any grit or sand. Dry thoroughly (the herbs shouldn't have even a drop of water on them).

- Chop the herbs finely (with adult help). Using a mezzaluna (as shown in the photo on the facing page).

### 3 Cooking the kuku

- Preheat oven to 400°F (200°C).

- Break the eggs into a large, shallow mixing bowl. Add the baking powder, advieh, salt, pepper, garlic, chopped herbs, fenugreek, flour, and ¼ cup of olive oil. Mix lightly with a large spoon. **Do not over-mix**.

- Oil a baking sheet and line it with parchment paper. Oil the parchment paper with ¼ cup of oil.

- Pour in the egg mixture and bake uncovered for 20 minutes.

- Using oven mitts, remove the baking sheet from the oven. Allow to cool.

- Cut the kuku into 3-inch-by-3-inch squares.

- To make the garnish: in a fine-mesh colander, rinse the barberries well with cold water.

- Use oven mitts. Heat a skillet over medium heat and add 2 tablespoons of oil and 2 tablespoons of sugar. Add the barberries and stir well for 20 seconds (be careful; barberries burn easily). Set aside.

- When ready to serve, use a spatula to sprinkle the barberries over the top of the kuku. Cut the kuku into squares and serve with yogurt, or yogurt and cucumber dip (page 67) on the side. Herb kuku is also good served with green rice and fish.

## ingredients

**dried chickpeas** ¼ cup dried, picked over

**kidney beans** ½ cup dried, picked over

**fresh dill** 1 cup washed, chopped

**fresh parsley** 1 cup washed, coarsely chopped

**baby spinach** fresh, 4 pounds; or **frozen chopped spinach** 1 pound

**vegetable oil** ½ cup

**onions** 4 large, peeled and thinly sliced

**garlic** 5 cloves, crushed and peeled

**coarse salt** 2 teaspoons

**black pepper** 1 teaspoon, freshly ground

**turmeric** 1 teaspoon

**chicken broth** or **water** 12 cups

**lentils** ½ cup

**Persian** or **linguine dried noodles** ½ pound

**fresh scallions** ½ cup, washed and coarsely chopped

**sun-dried yogurt** *(kashk)* 1 cup

GARNISH

**vegetable oil** 2 tablespoons

**garlic** 5 cloves, crushed, peeled, and chopped

**turmeric** 1 teaspoon

**dried mint flakes** ¼ cup, crushed

# Noodle Soup
## ASH-E RESHTEH

In Iran, noodles are traditionally served on Nowruz, when eating them symbolizes unraveling the difficulties of the year to come.

## 1 Before you start

- Gather all the ingredients and tools. Ask for adult help, especially for cutting and chopping vegetables and herbs, and using the stove top.

- In a large shallow bowl, soak the chickpeas and kidney beans in 4 cups of water for 30 minutes. Drain and set aside.

- In a large bowl of cold water, soak dill, parsley, and spinach for 15 minutes. Drain and repeat three times (herbs have lots of grit and sand that must be thoroughly washed out). Drain and allow to dry completely. Set aside.

## 2 Cooking the soup

- Place a large pot on a stove turned to medium heat. Add the oil and heat it. Add the onions and, using a long-handled spoon and an oven mitt, stir-fry for 10 minutes. Add the garlic, salt, pepper, turmeric, chickpeas, and kidney beans, and stir-fry for another minute.

- Pour in 12 cups of broth and bring to boil. Reduce heat to low, cover, and simmer for 45 minutes over medium heat.

- Add the lentils. Cover and cook for 20 minutes. Taste the beans to be sure they are cooked.

- Add the noodles and cook for 10 minutes, stirring occasionally.

- Add the sun-dried yogurt (kashk) and stir for 5 minutes using a long-handled silicone spoon.

- Add the dill, parsley, spinach, and scallions, and continue to cook, stirring from time to time, for 30 minutes.

- If the soup is too thick, add some of the remaining stock or warm water and bring back to a boil. Reduce heat to low, cover, and keep warm until ready to serve.

## 3 Making the garnish (na'na daq)

- To make the garnish, heat 2 tablespoons of oil in a medium skillet over medium heat. Add the garlic and stir-fry for 1 minute or until golden brown. Add the turmeric and stir for 20 seconds. Remove from heat, add the mint, and stir well. Set aside.

- Just before serving the soup, taste the soup and adjust seasoning to your taste. Add more salt or sun-dried yogurt (kashk) if needed.

- Pour the soup into individual bowls and place 1 teaspoon of the garnish in the center of each bowl.

MAKES: 4 SERVINGS

PREPARATION TIME: 15 MINUTES

COOKING TIME: NONE

## ingredients

**fresh mint** 2 tablespoons chopped

**fresh dill** 2 tablespoons, chopped

**fresh thyme** 1 tablespoon, chopped or **dried thyme** ½ teaspoon

**fresh tarragon** 4 tablespoons chopped; or **dried tarragon** ½ teaspoon

**yogurt** 3 cups plain whole or low-fat

**seedless cucumber** 1 long; or **pickling cucumbers** 4, peeled and grated

**scallions** ¼ cup, chopped

**dried organic rose petals,** 3 tablespoons, crushed

**garlic** 1 clove, crushed, peeled, and finely chopped

**shelled walnuts** ¼ cup, coarsely chopped

**raisins** ½ cup

**coarse salt** 2 teaspoons

**black pepper** ½ teaspoon, freshly ground

**pita bread** 2, toasted

## special tools

scissors and mezzaluna for cutting and chopping the herbs

grater

rubber spatula

# Yogurt and Cucumber Dip
## MAST-O KHIAR

## 1 Before you start

- Gather all the ingredients and tools. Ask for adult help when peeling and chopping the ingredients. A mezzaluna (below) simplifies chopping large quantities.

- Soak the mint, dill, thyme, and tarragon for 15 minutes in a large container of cold water. Drain and rinse three times to remove any grit or sand. Dry thoroughly.

## 2 Making the dip

- In a large, shallow mixing bowl, combine the yogurt, cucumber, scallions, mint, dill, thyme, tarragon, rose petals, garlic, walnuts, raisins, salt, and pepper.

- Mix thoroughly with a big spoon or rubber spatula and adjust seasoning to taste.

- Cover and allow to chill in the refrigerator.

- Serve with toasted pita or flatbread (page 57) and kuku (page 63).

## ingredients

**long-grain white basmati rice** 2 cups (for this recipe I like to use Ahoo Bareh basmati rice)

**olive oil** ½ cup

**onion** 1 large, peeled and thinly diced

**garlic** 2 cloves, peeled and crushed

**chicken (skinless, boneless thighs)** 1 pound, cut with the grain into 1-inch strips

**coarse salt** 1 tablespoon

**black pepper** 1 teaspoon, freshly ground

**advieh** (Persian spice mix) 1 teaspoon

**fresh lime juice** 2 tablespoons

**ground saffron threads** ½ teaspoon

**red chili pepper** ½ teaspoon (optional)

**French green beans, fresh or frozen** 1 pound, cleaned and cut into 2-inch pieces

**tomatoes, fresh** 4 large, sliced; or **canned tomatoes** 1 pound, drained

## special tools

a medium-sized rice cooker

long silicone spatula

Note: If you don't use basmati rice, washing the rice once is sufficient.

# Red Rice with Green Beans

## LUBIA POLOW

This dish was my childhood favorite; we called it red rice (because of the tomatoes in the rice). It was also my children's favorite when they were growing up. Whenever I asked them what they wanted, they would say *lubia polow.* I have included this recipe in memory of my childhood and theirs.

### 1 Before you start

- Gather all the ingredients and tools. Ask for adult help, especially for cutting and chopping vegetables, and using the rice cooker.

### 2 Washing the rice

- Pick over to remove any grit or bad grains. Wash the rice thoroughly by placing it in a large, shallow container filled with warm water. Gently pour off the water. Repeat five times until the water is quite clear. Drain in a fine-mesh colander and set aside.

### 3 Cooking the rice

- Turn on the medium-sized rice cooker. Add ½ cup of oil to the rice cooker pot. Add the onion, garlic, meat, salt, pepper, advieh, lime juice, saffron, and red chili pepper. Stir-fry for 7 minutes using a long silicone spatula.
- Add the green beans and stir-fry for 1 minute.
- Add the tomatoes, cover, and cook for 20 minutes.
- Add the rice and stir gently for 2 minutes to combine all the ingredients evenly.
- Cover and cook for 10 minutes.
- Remove the cover and stir gently. Cover again and continue to cook for another 10 minutes.
- Unplug the rice cooker and allow to cool, still covered, for 5 minutes.

### 4 Serving the rice

- Use oven mitts to remove the lid and transfer the rice to a serving platter.

MAKES: 4 SERVINGS

PREPARATION TIME: 45 MINUTES

COOKING TIME: 30 MINUTES

## ingredients

**long-grain white basmati rice** 2 cups

**fresh leeks** (white and green parts) 1 cup, washed and finely chopped

**fresh dill** 1½ cups, finely chopped or ½ cup dried

**fresh parsley** 1½ cup, finely chopped; or **dried parsley** ½ cup

**fresh cilantro** 1 cup finely chopped; or **dried cilantro** ¼ cup

**garlic** 2 cloves, crushed, peeled, and chopped

**vegetable oil** ½ cup

**cardamom pods** 3

**cinnamon stick** 1, 4-inches long

**coarse salt** 2 teaspoons

**water** 3 cups

**freshly ground saffron threads** ½ teaspoon, diluted in ¼ cup of hot water

## special tools

mezzaluna

medium-sized rice cooker

long silicone spatula

fine-mesh colander

# Green Rice

SABZI POLOW

## 1 Before you start

- Gather all the ingredients and tools. Ask for adult help, especially for cutting and chopping vegetables and herbs, and for using the rice cooker.

## 2 Washing the rice and herbs

- Place the rice in a large container and fill it with warm water. Gently pour off the water and repeat five times until the water is quite clear. Drain in a fine-mesh colander and set aside.

- Cut the leeks length-wise and soak in a large container of cold water for 15 minutes. Drain and dry thoroughly.

- Using the same container, soak the dill, parsley, and cilantro in cold water for 15 minutes. Drain and rinse. Repeat a few times. Dry the herbs thoroughly and chop (a mezzaluna simplifies the chopping).

## 3 Cooking the rice

- Place all the ingredients except the saffron water in the rice cooker and gently stir with a large wooden spoon or silicone spatula. Switch on the rice cooker and close the top.

- Cook for 15 minutes, then uncover and stir gently for 2 minutes. Add the saffron water.

- Cover and cook for 15 more minutes. Unplug the rice cooker and allow to cool, with the lid still closed, for 5 minutes to loosen the rice crust.

- Use oven mitts to transfer the rice to a serving platter. Serve with fish strips (page 73) and herb kuku (page 63).

71

MAKES: 4 SERVINGS
PREPARATION TIME: 15 MINUTES
COOKING TIME: 35 MINUTES

## ingredients

**vegetable oil** 2 tablespoons

**Ritz crackers** 1 cup

**skinless, boneless catfish**
2 pounds cut into 3-inch strips, rinsed and patted dry

**fresh lime juice** ¼ cup

**salt** 2 teaspoons

**black pepper** ½ teaspoon, freshly ground

**turmeric** 1 teaspoon

**garlic powder** 2 teaspoons

**paprika** ½ teaspoon

**all-purpose flour** ¼ cup

**egg whites** 2

GARNISH

**Seville orange (or lime)** 2

**Ketchup**

## special tools

parchment paper

freezer bag

rolling pin

whisk

VARIATION

You can replace the fish with 2 pounds of skinless chicken strips.

# Fish Strips
## MAHI-E TANURI

Traditionally, Iranians served smoked fish at Nowruz because there was no refrigeration in the old days. Now, you can serve any type of fish you prefer.

## 1 Before you start

- Gather all the ingredients and tools. Ask for adult help, especially for cutting and chopping vegetables and herbs, and for using the oven and stove top.

## 2 Preparing the fish strips

- Line a standard baking sheet with parchment paper.

- Brush the parchment paper with 2 tablespoons of oil. Set aside.

- Place the crackers in a large freezer bag, close, and beat the crackers with a rolling pin to break them up. Use the rolling pin to roll over the crackers and turn them into crumbs.

- Place 3 shallow bowls on the kitchen counter: one for the fish, one for the flour, and one for the egg whites.

- Place the fish strips in the first bowl and sprinkle with lime juice, salt, pepper, turmeric, garlic, and paprika. Toss gently so that the fish is covered with the mixture. Allow to rest for 10 minutes.

- Place the flour in the second bowl. Coat both sides of each fish strip, one at a time, with flour.

- In the third bowl, beat the egg whites with a whisk until frothy and dip the fish strips in, one at a time.

- Drop the fish strips into the freezer bag with the crumbs. When all the strips are in the bag, shake the bag so the fish is covered with crumbs. Transfer the crumb-coated fish strips onto the baking sheet lined with parchment paper, one at a time, and keep cool until ready to bake.

## 3 Cooking the fish strips

- When ready to bake, preheat oven to 400°F (200°C) and remove baking sheet of fish from the refrigerator.

- Bake for 30 to 35 minutes, or until golden brown.

- Use oven mitts to remove from oven.

- Dash with fresh Seville orange juice (or lime juice) and salt. Fresh Seville oranges are available at Iranian markets in spring.

- Serve with green rice (page 71) or Ketchup.

MAKES: 10 COOKIES

PREPARATION TIME: 15 MINUTES, PLUS 40 MINUTES RESTING TIME

COOKING TIME: 8 TO 10 MINUTES

## ingredients

**egg** 1

**vegetable oil** ½ cup

**molasses** ¼ cup

**honey** ¼ cup

**fresh ginger** 3-inch, grated

**brown sugar** ½ cup

**chili flakes** ½ teaspoon

**all-purpose unbleached flour** 3 cups

**baking powder** 2 teaspoons

**salt** ¼ teaspoon

**ground cinnamon** ½ teaspoon

### ICING

**you can make your own, below, or buy ready made**

**confectioners' sugar** 1½ cups

**water** 4 tablespoons

**food coloring** red

**raisins**

**candies**

**party sprinkles**

## special tools

rolling pin; baking mats; Haji Firuz cookie cutter*; 2 cooling racks; flat metal spatula

*If you don't have a Haji Firuz cookie cutter, use the Haji Firuz-shaped template on page 117 by tracing or cutting it out and placing it on the dough so that you can cut the dough around it with a sharp knife.

# Haji Firuz Gingerbread Cookies
## NUN-E GHANDI

### 1 Before you start
- Gather all the ingredients and tools and ask for adult help, especially when using the oven.

### 2 Making the dough
- In a large mixing bowl, combine the egg, oil, molasses, honey, ginger, sugar, and chili flakes, and whisk well.
- In a medium shallow mixing bowl, combine the flour, baking powder, salt, and cinnamon.
- Add the flour mixture to the egg mixture and knead with your hands until the dough forms (about 5 minutes).
- Divide the dough into 2 equal balls.
- Wrap each ball with plastic and refrigerate for 40 minutes.

### 3 Baking the cookies
- Preheat oven to 350°F (180°C).
- Line several baking sheets with baking mats.
- On a lightly floured surface use a rolling pin to roll out each ball to ¼-inch thickness.
- Place the Haji Firuz cookie cutter on the dough and punch out the shape by pressing straight down and lifting straight up.
- Use a flat spatula to gently lift up the shaped dough and place it on the baking sheet. Repeat this for all the dough. Be sure to leave at least 2 inches between each one. Cover with a towel to prevent the dough from drying.
- Place the baking sheet in the middle rack of your preheated oven and bake for about 8 to 10 minutes, until crispy on the outside.

- Using oven mitts, remove the baking sheet from the oven and set on a cooling rack for 10 minutes.
- With a flat metal spatula, gently lift each cookie off the baking sheet and place on a cooling rack to allow to cool completely.
- Continue with the next baking sheet.

### 4 Decorating the cookies
- To make the icing: in a shallow bowl, mix the confectioners' sugar with 4 tablespoons of water until smooth. Add a few drops of red to the bowl and mix until the icing is red.
- Smooth the icing on the body of the cookies and use raisins or candies for eyes, and/or any other of your favorite sprinkles for decoration.

MAKES: 12 CUPCAKES
PREPARATION TIME: 10 MINUTES
COOKING TIME: 25 MINUTES

## ingredients

**rice flour** ¼ cup

**all-purpose flour** 2 cups

**baking powder** 1 teaspoon

**baking soda** 1 teaspoon

**salt** ¼ teaspoon

**ground cardamom**
  1 tablespoon

**eggs** 4

**sugar** 1¼ cups

**unsalted butter** ½ cup

**yogurt** 1 cup

**cooking rose water**
  1 tablespoon

**sprinkles**

## special tools

rubber spatula

12 paper or silicone muffin
  cups

12-cup nonstick muffin pan

## optional icing

In a large shallow mixing
bowl, whisk 3 egg whites and
3 cups confectioners' sugar
for 5 minutes. Add
2 tablespoons freshly
squeezed lime juice and
continue whisking for another
2 minutes, until you have a
thick icing. Spoon icing over
the cupcakes and decorate
with fresh fruit or candies
(photo on facing page,
top right).

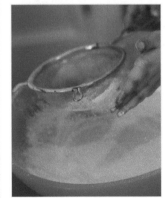

# Nowruz Cupcakes
## KEYK-E YAZDI

### 1 Before you start

- Gather all the ingredients and tools and ask for adult help, especially when using the oven.
- Preheat oven to 350°F (180°C).

### 2 Making the batter

- Sift together the rice flour, all-purpose flour, baking powder, baking soda, salt, and cardamom into a large shallow bowl.
- In another large shallow bowl, use a whisk to beat the eggs and sugar until creamy.
- Add the butter, yogurt and rose water and mix well until smooth.
- Using a long, rubber spoon, gradually add the dry ingredients to the wet ingredients. Mix, but do not over-mix (about 25 turns).

### 3 Decorating the cupcakes

- Place 12 paper muffin cups in the nonstick muffin pan.
- Spoon the batter into each paper muffin cup to about 2/3 full.
- Decorate each cupcake with your favorite sprinkles.

### 4 Baking the cupcakes

- Using oven mitts, place the muffin pan in the center of the oven.
- Bake for 25 minutes, or until lightly golden (if you stick a toothpick in the center of the cupcake and it comes out clean, your cupcakes are ready).
- Using oven mitts, remove the muffin pan from the oven. Take the cupcakes out of the pan and arrange on a cooling rack.
- Allow to cool completely. If you don't plan to eat the cupcakes right away, store them in a covered container in the refrigerator to keep them fresh.

### For gluten-free cupcakes

- Increase the rice flour to 1½ cups, and replace the all purpose flour with 1½ cups almond flour. Everything else remains the same.

### For dairy-free cupcakes

- Replace the yogurt with a mixture of the zest of 1 orange, ¼ cup juice of the same orange, and 1 apple, grated. Everything else remains the same.

MAKES: 18 CREAM PUFFS
PREPARATION TIME: 20 MINUTES
COOKING TIME: 40 MINUTES

## ingredients

### DOUGH

**unbleached all-purpose flour** 1 cup

**cold water** 1 cup

**salt** ¼ teaspoon

**unsalted butter** 6 tablespoons, diced into small pieces

**vanilla extract** 1 teaspoon

**eggs** 4, at room temperature

### FILLING

**heavy cream** 1 pint (chilled)

**sugar** 5 tablespoons

**rose water** 1 teaspoon

**orange zest** of 1 orange

### DUSTING

**confectioners' sugar** ¼ cup

## special tools

2 baking sheets

2 baking mats

wax paper

medium sauce pan with a handle

candy thermometer

ice cream scoop

### VARIATION

You may substitute your favorite ice cream flavor for the filling.

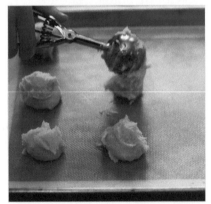

# Cream Puff
## NUN-E KHAMEYI

## 1 Before you start

- Gather all the ingredients and tools and ask for adult help, especially when using knives or the oven.
- Line 2 baking sheets with baking mats or parchment paper.
- Preheat oven to 425°F (220°C).

## 2 Dough

- Sift the flour onto a sheet of wax paper and set aside.
- In a heavy-based medium saucepan over medium heat, combine the water, salt, butter, and vanilla, and bring to a boil, stirring well with a wooden spoon.
- Reduce heat to **very low** and add the flour, all at once, stirring constantly, for 3 to 5 minutes, until you have a stiff paste.
- Use oven mitts to remove the saucepan from the heat.
- Continue to stir for another 4 to 5 minutes while the dough is cooling. The temperature of the mixture for the next stage is very important; use a candy thermometer to be sure it's around 150°F (65°C).
- Add 1 egg and stir for 1 minute. The dough becomes glossy and silky. Continue to stir for about another minute or until the egg has been absorbed and the dough is **no longer glossy.**
- Continue adding the eggs, one at a time, stirring each time an egg is added until the dough is no longer glossy (1 to 2 minutes).
- Add the last egg and stir until the dough is smooth, light, and airy, and no longer glossy.

## 3 Baking

- Use an ice cream scoop to drop scoops full of dough onto the prepared baking sheet, leaving 2 inches between each scoop to allow for expansion.
- **Using oven mitts and adult help,** place the baking sheet in the middle rack of the preheated oven. Bake for 20 minutes at 425°F (220°C).
- **Without opening the oven door,** reduce heat to 350°F (180°C) and continue to bake for 15 to 20 minutes, until the puffs are golden brown.
- **Using oven mitts and adult help,** remove the baking sheet from the oven, place on a cooling rack, and immediately poke each hot puff with a wooden stick to release the steam (to keep the puffs from becoming soggy).
- Allow to cool thoroughly, for about 15 minutes.

## 4 Filling

- Meanwhile, in a mixing bowl, whisk the cream, sugar, rose water, and orange zest until soft peaks form. Keep chilled.

## 5 Decorating and serving

- Using your hands or a knife break each puff into 2 halves.
- Use an ice cream scoop to fill half of the puff with the chilled filling. Place the other half on top. Repeat for all the puffs.
- Dust with confectioners' sugar and take a bite immediately – it's the cook's treat!
- Cover and refrigerate any cream puffs not eaten right away.

MAKES: 8 BUNS (4-INCH)
PREPARATION TIME: 20 MINUTES PLUS
1 HOUR RESTING TIME
COOKING TIME: 30 MINUTES

## ingredients

DOUGH

**all-purpose flour** 2½ cups

**ground cumin** 1 teaspoon

**baking powder** 1 teaspoon

**baking soda** ½ teaspoon

**wheat malt** 1½ cups

**butter** 1 cup, room temperature

**water** ½ cup

**honey** 2 tablespoons

**rose water** ¼ cup

FILLING

**pitted dates** 2 cups

**shelled walnuts** 1 cup

**shelled pistachios** 1 cup

**ground nutmeg** ½ teaspoon

**ground cardamom** 2 teaspoons

**ground cinnamon** ½ teaspoon

**oil** 1 tablespoon

**orange zest** of 1 orange

**sugar** 2 tablespoons

GLAZE

**corn oil** ½ cup

## special tools

rolling pin; baking mat; pastry brush; freezer bag; plastic wrap

Note: Wheat malt can be found in Iranian stores.

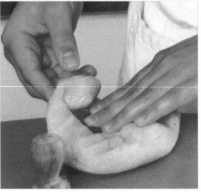
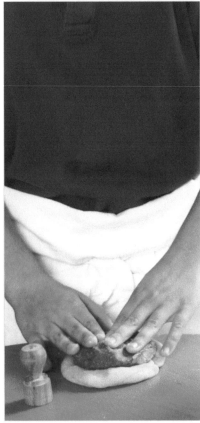

# Cinnamon Date Bun
## KOLUCHEH

### 1 Before you start

- Gather all the ingredients and tools. Ask for adult help, especially when using the oven.

### 2 Making the dough

- Sift the flour into a large shallow mixing bowl with ground cumin, baking powder, and baking soda.
- Add the wheat malt and butter and mix using your hands until you have a crumbly dough.
- Add the water, honey, and rose water. Knead well for 5 to 10 minutes, until you have a soft dough. Cover with plastic wrap and allow to rest at room temperature for 1 hour.

### 3 Making the filling

- Combine all the filling ingredients in a large freezer bag. Seal and beat the mixture with a rolling pin to break up the nuts. Roll over the nuts using the rolling pin until you have a soft paste. Divide the filling into 8 portions.

### 4 Filling the dough

- Divide the dough into 8 balls. In a cool, floured surface, roll out each ball into a ¼-inch-thick by 4-inch-round disk.
- Spread 1 portion of the filling over each of the 8 disks.
- Gently lift up each disk. Gather and pinch the edges to seal the filling inside. Turn disk over and gently press it down. A stamp can be used to decorate the top.

- Lay the filled buns 2 inches apart on a baking sheet lined with a baking mat. Using a pastry brush, generously brush each bun with oil. Repeat for a second baking sheet. Keep chilled until ready to cook.

### 5 Bake the buns

- Preheat the oven to 350°F (180°C).
- Using oven mitts, place the baking sheet in the center of the preheated oven. Bake for 25 to 30 minutes, until the buns are lightly brown.
- Remove from the oven and allow to cool on a cooling rack.
- Arrange in a basket and serve with tea. These buns will also keep well in an airtight container in the refrigerator.

MAKES: 20 COOKIES
PREPARATION TIME: 15 MINUTES
COOKING TIME: 10 TO 15 MINUTES

## ingredients

**unsalted butter or canola oil** 1 cup

**vanilla** 1 teaspoon

**sugar** 1¾ cups

**eggs** 4

**raisins, seedless** 2 cups

**all-purpose flour** 2 1/3 cups

## special tools

2 baking mats

whisk

rubber spatula

ice cream scoop

flat metal spatula

# Chewy Raisin Cookies
## NUN-E KESHMESHI

### 1 Before you start

- Gather all the ingredients and tools and ask for adult help, especially when using the oven.
- Preheat oven to 350°F (180°C).
- Spread out baking mat on a baking sheet.

### 2 Making the batter

- In a large mixing bowl, combine butter, vanilla, and sugar, and mix well.
- Add the eggs, one at a time. Whisk until creamy.
- Add raisins and mix well.
- Use a rubber spatula to fold in the flour until a soft dough forms.

### 3 Baking

- Use an ice cream scoop to scoop up the batter, dropping it onto the baking mat. Leave about 2 inches between each spoonful.
- Using oven mitts, place the baking sheet in the center of the oven and bake for 10 minutes, or until the cookies' edges are lightly golden brown. (If they are not, bake for another few minutes.)

### 4 Allowing cookies to cool

- Using oven mitts, remove the baking sheet from the oven and use a metal spatula to gently lift the cookies off the baking mat.
- Allow the cookies to cool for 5 minutes on a cooling rack. If you don't plan to eat the cookies right away, after they are cool, they can be stored in a cookie jar or an airtight plastic container.

MAKES: 20 COOKIES
PREPARATION TIME: 30 MINUTES
COOKING TIME: 15 TO 20 MINUTES

# ingredients

BATTER
**shelled walnuts** 4 cups
**egg yolks** 5
**confectioners' sugar** ¾ cup
**vanilla extract** 1 teaspoon

DECORATION
**chocolate kisses** 20

# special tools

2 baking sheets
2 baking mats
freezer bag
rolling pin
whisk
rubber spatula
ice cream scoop
flat metal spatula

# Walnut Kiss Cookies

NUN-E GERDUI

## 1 Before you start

- Gather all the ingredients and tools and ask for adult help, especially when using the oven.
- Preheat oven to 350°F (180°C).
- Place a baking mat on each baking sheet.

## 2 Making the batter

- Place the walnuts in a large freezer bag, close, and beat the nuts with a rolling pin to break them up. Now use the rolling pin to roll over the nuts and turn them into crumbs.
- In a mixing bowl, beat the egg yolks until creamy. Add the confectioners' sugar, vanilla, and walnuts. Mix thoroughly for a few minutes with a rubber spatula until a thick batter forms.

## 3 Baking and decorating

- Use an ice cream scoop to scoop up a rounded spoonful of the batter. Drop the batter on the baking mat, leaving about 2½ inches between the cookies. Press down.
- Unwrap some chocolate kisses and place one in the center of each cookie.
- Using oven mitts, place the baking sheet in the center rack of the preheated oven and bake for 15 to 20 minutes until the edges of the cookies are brown.

- Using oven mitts, remove the baking sheet from the oven and place it on a cooling rack. Lift the cookies off the mat with a metal spatula and arrange the cookies on another cooling rack.
- Repeat step 3 for the second baking sheet.
- If you don't plan to eat the cookies right away, they can be stored in a cookie jar or an airtight plastic container after they are cool.

## ingredients

BATTER

**blanched almonds** 4 cups
  (1 pound)

**egg whites** 5

**confectioners' sugar**
  1½ cups

**ground cardamom** ½
  teaspoon or **rose water**
  2 tablespoons

DECORATION

**almond drage** 20

**candies and sprinkles**

## special tools

2 baking sheets

2 baking mats

rolling pin

freezer bag

whisk

rubber spatula

ice cream scoop

flat metal spatula

# Almond Candy Cookies

NUN-E BADAMI

## 1 Before you start

- Gather all the ingredients and tools and ask for adult help, especially when using the oven.
- Preheat oven to 350°F (180°C).
- Place baking mats on the two baking sheets.

## 2 Making the batter

- Place the almonds in a large freezer bag, close, and beat the nuts with a rolling pin to break them up. Now use the rolling pin to roll over the nuts and turn them into a granulated powder.
- In a mixing bowl, beat the egg whites until foamy. Add the sugar, almond, and cardamom. Mix and scrape down with a rubber spatula until a thick batter is formed.

## 3 Decorating

- Using an ice cream scoop, scoop out some of the batter and place it on the baking mat. Continue, leaving 2½ inches between each piece for expansion.
- Decorate each piece with an almond drage candy.

## 4 Baking

- Using oven mitts, place the baking sheet in the center of the oven and bake for about 15 to 20 minutes, until the cookies' edges are golden brown.
- Using oven mitts, remove the baking sheet from the oven. Use a metal spatula to remove the cookies from the baking sheet and place on a cooling rack.
- Allow the cookies to cool on the cooling rack.
- Repeat step 3 for the second baking sheet.
- If you don't plan to eat the cookies right away, they can be stored in a cookie jar or an airtight plastic container after they are cool.

MAKES: **20** PIECES

PREPARATION TIME: **30** MINUTES

PLUS **1** TO **2** HOURS FOR SYRUP TO COOL

COOKING TIME: **15** TO **20** MINUTES

## ingredients

SYRUP

**sugar** 1½ cups

**water** ½ cup

**rose water** ¼ cup

**fresh lime juice** ¼ teaspoon

BATTER

**egg yolks** 4

**canola oil** 1 cup

**cardamom powder** 1½
  teaspoons

**rice flour** 3 cups

**syrup** (made in step 2)

DECORATION

**poppy seeds** 2 tablespoons

**sprinkles,** your favorite ones

## special tools

2 baking sheets

2 baking mats

whisk

rubber spatula

plastic wrap

flat metal spatula

ice cream scoop

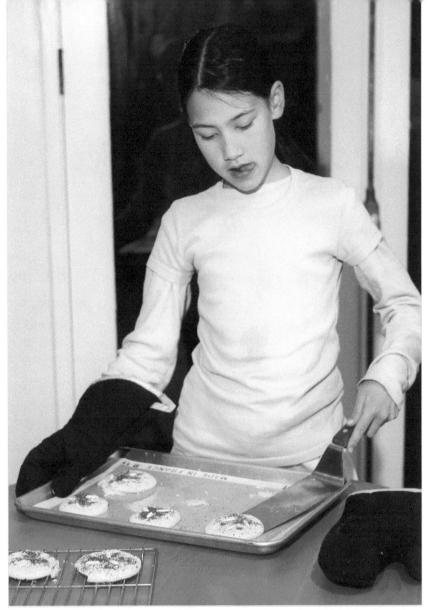

# Rice Cookies
## NUN-E BERENJI

### 1 Before you start

- Gather all the ingredients and tools and ask for adult help, especially when using the oven.

### 2 Preparing the syrup

- Combine sugar and water in a small saucepan. Bring to a boil, stir once and allow to **simmer for 2 minutes** (be careful not to over-boil).

- Using oven mitts, remove saucepan from heat, add rose water and lime juice, and set aside to cool. Syrup should be at room temperature and **not hot.**

### 3 Making the dough

- In a mixing bowl, beat the egg yolks until creamy. Add the syrup (at room temperature) made in step 2 and mix well.

- In another mixing bowl, combine oil, cardamom, and rice flour. Mix well for a few minutes. This will create a snow-white dough.

- Add the egg yolk mixture and fold in with a rubber spatula, until a soft dough forms (do not over-mix).

- Cover with plastic wrap and allow the dough to cool in the refrigerator for 30 minutes.

### 4 Decorating

- Preheat oven to 350°F (180°C).

- Line the baking sheets with baking mats.

- Take dough out of the refrigerator.

- Using an ice cream scoop, take a spoonful of dough, roll it into a ball the size of a walnut, flatten slightly, and place on the baking sheet.

- Repeat, leaving 2½ inches between each ball. With a fork, draw geometric patterns on the cookies and sprinkle with poppy seeds and your favorite sprinkles.

### 5 Baking

- Using oven mitts, place the baking sheet in the center of the preheated oven.

- Bake the cookies for 10 to 15 minutes (they should be white when done).

- Using oven mitts, remove the baking sheet from the oven and allow to cool on a rack.

- Repeat from step 4 for the second baking sheet.

- These cookies crumble very easily; remove them carefully from the baking sheet with a metal spatula and allow to cool on a cooling rack.

MAKES: **25** BERRIES

PREPARATION TIME: **30** MINUTES

COOKING TIME: NONE

## ingredients

PASTE

**ground almonds** 1½ to
2½ cups (you can also use
almond powder, sometimes
called almond flour)

**ground cardamom**
1 teaspoon

**confectioners' sugar** 1 cup

**rose water** 2 tablespoons

**orange-flower water**
1 tablespoon

**food coloring** red

FROSTING

**sugar** 1 cup

**pistachios** 2 tablespoons,
sliced (for stems)

## special tools

parchment paper

small, sharp knife

airtight shallow plastic
container

90

# Sweet Almond Berries

TUT

## 1 Before you start

- Gather all the ingredients and tools and ask for adult help, especially when using sharp knives.

## 2 Making the paste

- In a shallow mixing bowl, mix 1½ cups of ground almonds, cardamom, and confectioners' sugar.

- Using your hands, slowly blend in the rose water and orange-flower water, mixing constantly to make a soft paste. Add more ground almonds if necessary (the paste should not stick to your hands).

## 3 Preparing the berries

- Spread a sheet of parchment paper on the kitchen counter.

- Divide the paste evenly into 2 balls. Add a few drops of red food coloring to one of the balls of paste and knead it in until the paste is reddish.

- Roll each ball of paste into 1-inch-diameter tubes.

- Use a sharp knife to cut the rolls into 1-inch-long sections. Shape each section into a berry.

- Pour a cup of sugar onto a flat dish. Roll each berry in sugar until coated evenly.

- Insert a sliver of a pistachio on top of each berry so it looks like a stem.

- Arrange in a plastic container and cover tightly to keep berries from drying out.

- Place in the freezer until you are ready to serve. It will taste like a cold, fresh, yummy berry.

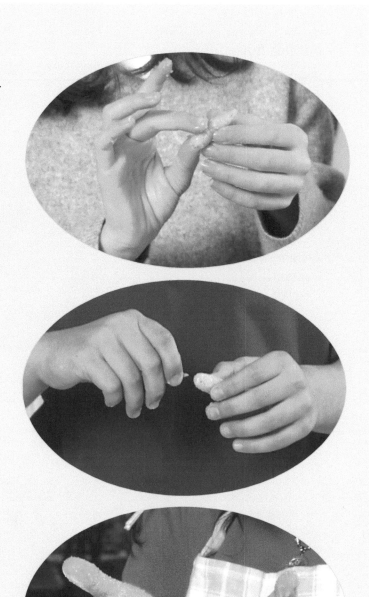

MAKES: ABOUT 40 COOKIES

PREPARATION TIME: 25 MINUTES PLUS
30 MINUTES RESTING

COOKING TIME: 15 MINUTES

## ingredients

**clarified butter or oil** 1 cup

**confectioners' sugar**
1½ cups

**cardamom powder** 4
teaspoons

**rose water** 1 tablespoon

**roasted chickpea flour\***
3–4½ cups, sifted

DECORATION

**unsalted, slivered
pistachios** or your favorite
**party sprinkles**

## special tools

sifter

baking mats

baking sheets

plastic wrap

clover leaf cookie cutter

\*There are two kinds of
chickpea flour in Iranian
markets. Make sure you buy
the one labeled "fine" (it is
roasted and specially made
for pastries).

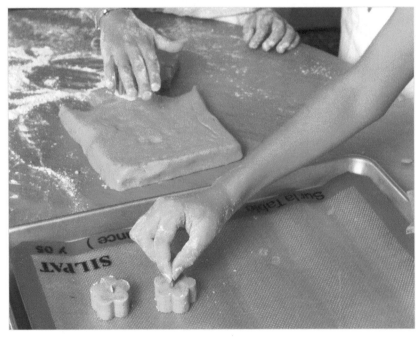

# Four-Leaf Clover Cookies
## NUN-E NOKHODCHI

## 1 Before you start

- Gather all the ingredients and tools and ask for adult help, especially when using the oven.

## 2 Making the dough

- In a large bowl, combine oil, sugar, cardamom, and rose water, and mix for 2 minutes until white and creamy.

- Add 3 cups chickpea flour all at once and mix for 1 minute, until you have a soft, sticky dough.

- Dust work surface with chickpea flour, knead dough 2 minutes by hand, add more chickpea flour if necessary, until dough is no longer sticky. Flatten it evenly on the work surface until it is 6 inches square and ¾-inch thick. Cover with plastic wrap and allow to rest at room temperature for 30 minutes.

## 3 Decorating

- Preheat oven to 300°F (150°C).
- Place baking mats on the baking sheets.
- Unwrap the dough.
- Dust a small clover leaf cookie cutter and use it to cut out the dough. Dust the cookie cutter with chickpea flour each time you cut out a new cookie.
- Place on the baking sheets, leaving 1 inch between pieces to allow them to expand in the oven. Decorate each cookie with slivered pistachios or your favorite sprinkles.

## 4 Baking

- Using oven mitts, place the baking sheet in the center of the oven and bake for 15 minutes. Using oven mitts, remove the baking sheet from the oven, place it on a cooling rack, and allow to cool. Repeat for the second baking sheet.

- These cookies are very delicate and crumble easily. They should be completely cool before handling. If you are not planning to serve them the same day, store them in an airtight glass container in the fridge.

MAKES: 1 TRAY

PREPARATION TIME: 15 MINUTES

COOKING TIME: 20 MINUTES

## ingredients

**sugar** 1 cup

**pure honey** 3 tablespoons

**vegetable oil** ¼ cup

**ground saffron** ¼ teaspoon

**rose water** 2 tablespoons

**blanched almonds** 1½ cups, unsalted and slivered

DECORATION

**pistachios** 2 tablespoons, unsalted and chopped

## special tools

parchment paper

baking sheet

long silicone spatula

flat metal spatula

candy thermometer

# Honey Almond Candy Crunch
## SOHAN ASALY

## 1 Before you start

- Gather all the ingredients and tools and ask for adult help, especially when using the stove top.
- Spread a piece of parchment paper over a baking sheet.

## 2 Making the candy

- Heat a large, nonstick skillet with a handle over medium heat.
- Add the sugar, honey, and oil and cook for 1 minute, stirring occasionally with a long silicone spatula.
- Add the saffron, rose water, and almonds to the skillet. Stir with the spatula from time to time while cooking for 15 to 20 minutes over medium heat, or until the mixture is firm and has a golden brown color. Be careful: It should not be dark brown.

- The candy is ready if candy thermometer shows 320°F (160°C), or if you drop a spoonful of the hot almond mixture into a bowl of ice water and it hardens immediately.
- Use oven mitts to remove the skillet from the heat immediately.

## 3 Finishing the candy

- Spread the hot candy over the parchment paper using the spatula to spread and flatten the candy.
- While still hot, sprinkle the chopped pistachios over the top of the candy.
- Allow the candy to cool, then break it into pieces. Remove from the paper.

## 4 Serving and storing

- Arrange candy on a serving platter, or to store it, keep in an airtight container or freezer bag in the freezer.

MAKES: 1 BAKING SHEET OF BAKLAVA
PREPARATION TIME: 35 MINUTES
COOKING TIME: 35 MINUTES

## ingredients

### SYRUP

**sugar** 2½ cups

**water** 1½ cups

**rose water** ½ cup

**fresh lime juice** 2 tablespoons

### FILLING

**blanched almonds** 2 pounds, ground (or use store-bought almond powder)

**sugar** 2 cups

**ground cardamom** 2 tablespoons

### DOUGH

**plain milk** ¼ cup

**corn** or **canola oil** ½ cup

**cool syrup** 1 tablespoon (prepared in step 2)

**rose water** ¼ cup

**egg** 1

**all-purpose flour** 2½ cups sifted

**corn oil** ¼ cup

### DECORATION

**pistachios** 2 tablespoons, chopped or ground

**almonds** 2 tablespoons, slivered

**rose petals** or **party sprinkles** 2 tablespoons

## special tools

whisk; plastic wrap; baking sheet; parchment paper; rolling pin; pastry brush

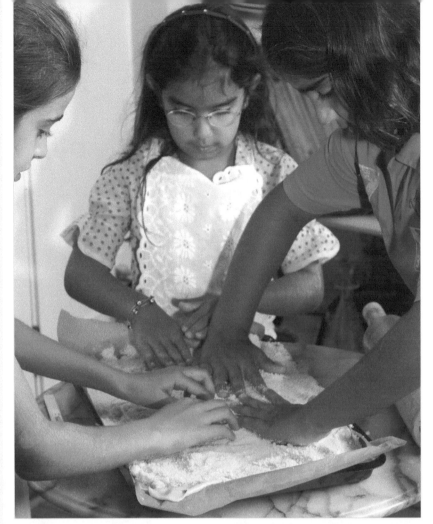

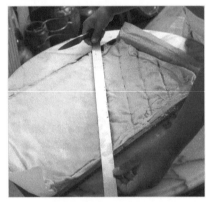

# Baklava
## BAQLAVA

## 1 Before you start

- Gather all the ingredients and tools and ask for adult help, especially when using the oven and stove top.
- Line a baking sheet with parchment paper and preheat the oven to 350°F (180°C).

## 2 Making the syrup

- Prepare the syrup by combining the sugar, water, rose water, and lime juice in a medium saucepan. Bring to a boil, stirring with a whisk. Using oven mitts, remove from heat and set aside.

## 3 Making the filling

- In a large, shallow mixing bowl, blend the almonds, sugar, and cardamom together. Set aside.

## 4 Making the dough

- In another large shallow mixing bowl, combine the milk, oil, 1 tablespoon cool syrup, rose water, and egg, and whisk well.
- Add the flour and knead well with your hands for 5 to 10 minutes to form dough (it should not stick to your hands).
- Divide the dough into 2 balls of equal size and wrap each in plastic.

## 5 Making the baklava

- Prepare a large, wide area for rolling out the dough. Dust the surface with flour. Unwrap 1 ball of dough from the plastic and roll out into a very thin rectangle with a rolling pin. The sheet of dough should be large enough to overlap the baking sheet.
- Transfer the dough to the lined baking sheet. Do not cut off the excess dough.
- Evenly spread the filling over the dough and smooth it. It is important to press down all over dough with your hands at this stage; it will help with the cutting later on.
- Roll out the second ball of dough and place it on top of the filling. Press down on the dough evenly with your hands all over the dough's surface.
- Press together and pinch the top and bottom edges of the overhanging dough to seal like a pie, forming a rim around the edge of the baking sheet.
- Use a sharp knife and a ruler or straight edge to cut a grid of 2-inch diamond shapes (see picture, on facing page).
- With a pastry brush, paint the dough with 2 tablespoons of oil. Using oven mitts, place the baking sheet in the middle of the preheated oven.

## 6 Baking and decorating

- Bake for 30 to 35 minutes, until the baklava is golden.
- Using oven mitts, remove the baking sheet from the oven. Pour **2/3** of the syrup over the top (keep the remainder for later use or in case some prefer their baklava with more syrup).
- Decorate the baklava with chopped or ground pistachios and almonds, rose petals, or your favorite sprinkles. Cover tightly with aluminum foil and let stand for 2 hours until it cools and settles.
- Lift the diamond pieces out of the baking pan and carefully arrange on a serving dish.
- Keep the baklava covered with aluminum foil to prevent it from drying out, and store in the refrigerator.

MAKES: **12** PASTRIES

PREPARATION TIME: **30** MINUTES

COOKING TIME: **10** MINUTES

## ingredients

**puff pastry sheets** 1 package
(2 ready-to-bake sheets),
thawed for 40 minutes at
room temperature

GLAZE

**baking soda** 1 teaspoon

**corn starch** 2 teaspoons

**confectioners' sugar**
1 tablespoon

**water** ½ cup

FLOUR-SUGAR COATING

**flour** 2 teaspoons

**confectioners' sugar** ½ cup

**granulated sugar** ½ cup

**butter** ½ cup, melted

DUSTING

**confectioners' sugar**
½ cup mixed with 1
teaspoon **cardamom
powder**

## special tools

2 baking sheets
parchment paper
rolling pin
pastry brush
cooling rack
sieve

# Puff Pastry Tongues
## ZABAN

## 1 Before you start

- Gather all the ingredients and tools and ask for adult help, especially when using the oven and stove top.

- Preheat the oven to 400°F (200°C).

- Line the baking sheets with parchment paper.

- Melt the butter in a small saucepan over low heat. Using oven mitts, remove the saucepan from the heat.

## 2 Making the glaze

- Place the baking soda, corn starch, sugar, and water in a small bowl, and stir with a fork until smooth.

## 3 Preparing the tongues

- Dust an area on the kitchen counter with 1 teaspoon flour, 1 tablespoon confectioners' sugar, and 1 tablespoon granulated sugar.

- Unfold one sheet of the thawed puff pastry over the flour and sugar surface on the counter.

- Dust evenly over the unfolded puff pastry with 1 tablespoon of confectioners' sugar and 1 tablespoon of granulated sugar. Use a rolling pin to lightly roll out the pastry.

- Paint the pastry evenly with melted butter.

- Fold the pastry in half lengthwise, from one end to the other.

## 4 Cutting and Glazing

- Cut the folded sheet of puff pastry into six 6-inch-by 2½-inch triangular strips.

- Round out the sharp ends of the triangle.

- Place the tongues on the prepared baking sheets, leaving 2 inches between each one.

- Gently paint the glaze evenly on each piece of the pastry.

- Sprinkle the remaining sugar over the tongues.

## 5 Baking

- Using oven mitts, place the baking sheet in the preheated oven and bake for about 10 to 14 minutes, or until golden.

- Using oven mitts, remove the baking sheet from the oven, and allow to cool on a cooling rack for 10 minutes.

- Continue with the next sheet of puff pastries.

- Use a sieve to dust the tongues with confectioners' sugar and cardamom powder.

MAKES: **12** POPSICLES
PREPARATION TIME: **15** MINUTES
COOKING TIME: NONE
SETTING TIME: **2** HOURS

## ingredients

**pomegranate juice** 4 cups

**sugar** ½ cup

**fresh lime juice**
2 tablespoons

**pomegranate seeds**
(optional) 1 cup (about
1 pomegranate)

**light corn syrup**
2 tablespoons

## special tools

popsicle mold
wooden sticks

---

### TO MAKE SORBET

Pour the mixture made in
step 2 into an ice cream
machine and run it for
40 minutes (follow the
manufacturer's instructions).

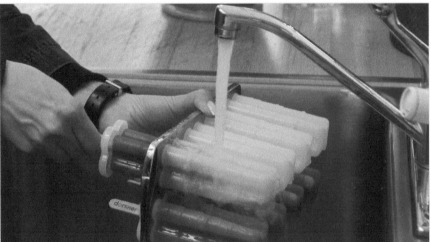

# Pomegranate Popsicles
## ALASKA-YE ANAR

### 1 Before you start

- Gather all the ingredients and tools. Ask for adult help.

### 2 Making the popsicles

- In a shallow mixing bowl or a pitcher that has a pour spout, mix all the ingredients until the sugar has dissolved.

- Pour into a popsicle mold and cover.
- Place the popsicle sticks in the slots.
- Place mold in the freezer. Let it sit for about 2 hours, or until firm.

### 3 Serving the popsicles

- Remove mold from freezer, rinse for a few seconds under warm running water, then jiggle to remove the popsicles.

MAKES: 1 PINT

PREPARATION TIME: 25 MINUTES

COOKING TIME: 15 MINUTES

MAKING TIME: 1 HOUR PLUS 1 HOUR

## Ingredients

CRUNCHY FROZEN CREAM

**thick cream** 1 cup

ICE CREAM

**sahlab mixture** 4 tablespoons (Cortas brand)

**whoe milk** 3 cups

**heavy cream** 1 cup

**sugar** 1 cup

**salt** ¼ teaspoon

**saffron** ¼ teaspoon threads dissolved in 2 tablespoons cooking **rose water**

**mastic** ½ teaspoon ground in a mortar and pestle with 1 teaspoon **sugar**

**pistachios** ¼ cup, unsalted, shelled, and broken up

SANDWICH WAFERS

Use ready-made round ice cream wafers, or cut out your own from a wafer sheet using a cookie cutter, or use your favorite cookies in this book (mine are raisin cookies, which should be wrapped in plastic and placed in the freezer until ready to use for an ice cream sandwich).

## special tools

parchment paper

mortar and pestle

ice cream maker

ice cream scoop

## 1 Before you start

- Gather all the ingredients and tools. Ask for adult help.

## 2 Making the crunchy cream

- Pour the thick cream into a 4-by-6-inch dish lined with parchment paper and place in the freezer

## 3 Making the ice cream

- In a small bowl dissolve the sahlab in 1 cup of cold milk and mix until quite smooth. Set aside.

- In a medium saucepan, combine 2 cups of milk, 1 cup of cream, and the sugar and bring to a boil. Ask for adult help when handling the hot saucepan.

- Add the sahlab mixture, salt, saffron mixture, and mastic and bring back to a boil.

- Reduce heat and simmer, whisking constantly, for 10 to 15 minutes, until thick enough for it to coat the back of a spoon.

- Remove from heat and allow to cool completely.

- Pour the mixture into the ice cream machine's container.

- Follow the instructions for the ice cream machine.

- Start the machine and run it for about 1 hour.

- Remove the frozen cream from the freezer. Break it up into ¼-inch pieces and add it to the ice cream in the machine. Add the pistachios and continue to turn in the machine for another 20 seconds.

- Transfer the ice cream into a plastic container with a press-in-place lid. Cover tightly (uncovered ice cream develops an unpleasant taste). Freeze the ice cream for at least 1 hour to allow it to develop texture and flavor.

# Cream Crunch
# Ice Cream Sandwich

## BASTANI-E NUNI

### 4 Assembling ice cream sandwich

- Twenty minutes before serving, remove the ice cream from the freezer and refrigerate. It should be soft for scooping.

- Place 2 scoops of ice cream on a wafer or on the flat side of a cookie (from the freezer) and place another wafer or cookie on top. Wrap in plastic and place in the freezer for 2 hours, or until the ice cream sandwich is firm.

MAKES: 1 QUART SYRUP, 1 PINT JAM
PREPARATION TIME: 15 MINUTES
COOKING TIME: 35 MINUTES

## ingredients

**sour cherries**
  3 pounds
  (pitted or unpitted)

**sugar** 5 cups

**fresh lime juice**
  4 tablespoons

**vanilla bean** 1, or
  ½ teaspoon **pure
  vanilla extract**

**water** 3 cups

## special tools

cheesecloth
jar with cover
bottle with cork

# Sour Cherry Cooler
## SHARBAT-E ALBALU

### 1 Before you start

- Gather all the ingredients and tools. Ask for adult help.

### 2 Preparing the cherries

- In a large colander rinse the sour cherries.
- Spread 2 layers of cheesecloth on the counter and dump the cherries on the cheesecloth.
- Stem the cherries and discard any blemished ones.

### 3 Making the syrup

- In a large pan, bring sugar, lime juice, vanilla, and 3 of cups water to a boil, stirring occasionally.
- Tie up the cherries in the cheesecloth and gently lower into the pan. Cook over medium heat for 35 minutes. Turn off the heat and allow to cool.
- Lift cherries in their cheesecloth and hold above pan for a minute to let syrup drain. The syrup in the pan will be saved as syrup and the cherries in the bundle as a jam or spread (delicious in Persian tea or with yogurt as a yummy dessert).
- Place the bundle in a large bowl and transfer the cherries to a jar for jam. Cover tightly and refrigerate for later use.
- Pour syrup into a clean bottle using a funnel. Cork tightly. Refrigerate until needed.

### 4 Making the cooler

- Stir 3 parts cold water with 1 part syrup in your favorite glass and add ice to make sour

continued on next page

## 4 Making the cooler (continued)

cherry coolers. Syrup can also be diluted with fizzy water to make cherry soda. When in season top the glass with a bunch of fresh cherries, sour or sweet.

## Tea with sour cherry jam

- Place 2 or 3 spoonfuls of the cherry jam in your tea instead of sugar to make a delicious tea.
- Drink the tea and eat the cherries using a spoon.

## Yogurt with sour cherry jam

- Place 2 or 3 spoonfuls of the cherry jam over some thick yogurt to make a delicious dessert.

# A New Year Is Born

Use this calendar appendix for a better understanding of the relationship between the earth's seasons, the Iranian and Western calendars and the Persian New Year.

Every Nowruz preparation builds up to the moment of the vernal equinox, which in Iranian households is a time for meditation and prayer. Tradition says that this is when guardian angels and ancestral spirits descend to earth, and all must be ready to receive them so that the New Year may begin serenely.

The list below shows the precise time in March that the sun will cross the celestial equator for the next four years. Times are given in Universal Standard Time, also known as Greenwich Mean Time. The Nowruz transition itself always begins at the exact moment of the equinox. The official Iranian calendar is set according to the time of the equinox: If it falls before noon Tehran time, that day becomes the first of the New Year; if it falls after noon, the next day is the first official day of the calendar year.

Because Universal Standard Time is set at the Greenwich Meridian in England, hours and minutes must be adjusted for different time zones around the world. To calculate the moment of equinox if you live in Iran, add five and a half hours to the times shown in the list; in the United States, for Eastern Daylight Saving Time (DST), subtract four hours; for Central DST, subtract five hours; for Mountain DST, subtract six hours; and for Pacific DST, subtract seven hours.

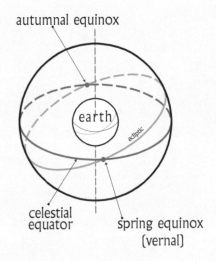

## The Vernal Equinox (Universal Standard Time)

2015 (1394 Iranian year): March 20, 10:45 pm     2017 (1396): March 20, 10:29 am

2016 (1395): March 20, 04:30 am     2018 (1397): March 20, 04:15 pm

The moment when the sun's path crosses the celestial equator moving north occurs around March 20. In the earth's northern hemisphere this is the vernal equinox, when day and night are of equal length, and spring is ushered in by Nowruz. The days lengthen and warm until about June 21, the summer solstice, when the day is longest and the sun is at its farthest point north of the celestial equator. As the sun moves on, the days shorten until about September 23, the autumnal equinox, when the sun crosses the celestial equator once more, and day and night are again of equal length. The days become shorter and the nights longer until about December 21, when the sun is at its farthest south of the celestial equator. This is the winter solstice, the briefest day of the year. (In the southern hemisphere, the seasons are reversed.)

The precise times for the earth's seasons can be found on the Naval Observatory website at: http://aa.usno.navy.mil/data/docs/EarthSeasons

# The Iranian Year – Counting the Days
## LUNAR AND SOLAR CALENDARS

**The calendar Iranians** use to record the past, arrange future events, and determine the dates of festivals such as Nowruz is, like Western calendars, based on the solar year (see graphic on page 110). It is the result of thousands of years of astronomers' calculations and corrections. And, like Nowruz itself, it is rich with echoes of Iran's long history.

The first calendars appeared in Mesopotamia at least 4,500 years ago. They were probably lunar calendars, because the cycle of the moon – from the first thin crescent to the last – was easy for the ancients to observe. But the seasons are based on a solar year, which makes the year eleven days longer than a lunar year. The lunar calendar's shortfall in days made planning difficult for farmers, priests, and governments, because it meant that the months gradually slipped behind the seasons. (The effect can be seen today in religious periods such as Ramadan, which is determined by a lunar calendar, and the Christian Easter, which is based on lunar–solar calculations. Both are celebrated on different dates each year.)

The ancients, therefore, made calendars that mixed solar and lunar observations. This was the kind of calendar first used by the Persians, and it was followed until the Arab conquests of the seventh century, when Persia adopted the Arabian lunar calendar (which had the same problems as all lunar calendars).

But astronomy was making advances in Iran. In 1079, eight astronomers working for Sultan Jalal el-Dowla – among them the mathematician Omar Khayyam, better known in the West for his poetry – devised what is now known as the Jalali, or Persian, calendar, basing it on the solar year.

This solar calendar functions much like the Gregorian calendar of the West, which was developed under Julius Caesar and reformed several times, most notably by sixteenth-century astronomers working for Pope Gregory XIII, who gave the calendar its name. There are important differences, though. For one thing, the Gregorian calendar begins with 1 CE, the year assigned as the date of Jesus' birth; the Persian calendar starts counting time from

622 CE on the Gregorian calendar, the year of the prophet Mohammad's flight from Mecca. For another, the Persian year begins on Nowruz, the spring equinox in March. Western cultures initially began the year in March as well – and Britain and its colonies continued to do so for hundreds of years. The Anglo-Saxons were out of step with their neighbors, however. Other Western countries had long begun the year on January 1, because officials of the Roman Empire traditionally assumed office on that date. In 1752, Britain and the United States switched to January 1.

There's another cultural difference as well. After the Mongols invaded Iran in the thirteenth century, Persians began to name their years after the animals of the twelve-year Asian cycle.

So the Iranian calendar – officially adopted along with the Asian zodiacal cycle of years during the Constitutional Revolution in 1911 – is a tapestry of traditions. Because its year begins with the vernal equinox, it coincides with the astronomical and astrological calendars, so that each Iranian month has an astrological sign. Iran inherited traditional astrology from ancient Babylon, and it's as popular among Persians as it is in the rest of the world. However, deep cultural memories were captured in the names Iranians gave their months.

## PERSIAN AND GREGORIAN CALENDARS HISTORICAL TIMELINE

# Naming the Months

**In most cultures, units of time** – hours, days, months, years – are named for forgotten gods or festivals. The Anglo-Saxon Thursday, for instance, commemorates Thor, the Norse thunder god; July was named in honor of Julius Caesar.

In this realm, the Iranian calendar is special. Although it was developed in the eleventh century, the names of its months come from those of deities that flourished from the sixth century BCE to the fourth century CE, when the vast Persian empires stretched from the Black Sea to the Persian Gulf and from the Nile River to the Indus.

The Iranians had long worshipped Ahura Mazda, the "Lord of Wisdom," as first among gods, but around 600 BCE, and possibly centuries earlier, the prophet Zoroaster had a great vision of a dualistic creation, in which Ahura Mazda, the supreme creative deity, font of light, virtue, and truth, battled Angra Mainyu, the "Hostile Spirit," lord of darkness, evil, and lies.

The tenth month of the Iranian calendar is named for the creator and the rest are named after the hosts of angelic beings he created. These beings, both deities in themselves and aspects of Ahura Mazda's divine nature, fought for truth and goodness against Angra Mainyu and his demons.

The first of these were the six Amesha Spanta, who with the Lord of Wisdom formed the Seven Immortals and guarded all of creation: sky, waters, earth, fire, plants, animals, and humans. As described on page 112, half the Iranian months – Ordibehesht, Khordad, Mordad, Shahrivar, Bahman, and Esfand – bear their names. The month of Dey was dedicated to the Lord of Wisdom.

The next group were the Yazata (Eyzad), or "Beings Worthy of Worship." There were hundreds, one for every good force in nature. The months of Tir, Mehr, Aban, and Azar honor different Yazata.

Last came the Forouhars, created by Ahura Mazda to protect all that lived. Among them were the Faravashi, guardian angels just for humans. The name of the first month – Farvardin – commemorates the angels' descent to earth to commune with humanity. Even now, there are Nowruz customs that recall this tradition.

The names and characters of the Iranian months, the Western dates they correspond to, and the zodiacal signs they bear are these:

**FARVARDIN**. This joyful month of Nowruz takes its name from the Faravashi, who were said to descend to earth at each New Year to bless and help the humans they watched over. Farvardin's dates in the West are March 21 to April 20; its astrological sign is Aries, the ram.

**ORDIBEHESHT**. The second month commemorates the ancient deity of fire and noonday heat, whose name signified ultimate righteousness. Ordibehesht's Western dates are April 21 to May 21; its astrological sign is Taurus, the bull.

**KHORDAD**. This month's name echoes one meaning – "health" or "wholeness" – that was given to a deity who protected the waters. Its Western dates are May 22 to June 21; its astrological sign is Gemini, the twins.

**TIR**. The fourth month is named for a god that originated in Babylon as Guardian of the Rains and Lord of the Scribes and of the planet Mercury. The name meant "the swift one." Tir's Western dates are June 22 to July 22; its astrological sign is Cancer, the crab.

**MORDAD**. This month's name, which means "death," has deteriorated over the centuries. The word should be Amordad or "immortality," because it honors a Zoroastrian deity who watched over all plant life. Mordad's Western dates are July 23 to August 22; its astrological sign is Leo, the lion.

**SHAHRIVAR**. The sixth month commemorates the lord of the sky, all stones, metals, and warriors; he protected the poor and the weak, and his name meant "the desirable dominion." Shahrivar's Western dates are August 23 to September 22; its astrological sign is Virgo, the virgin.

**MEHR**. In modern Persian, Mehr means "love and friendship." The source of the name is Mithra, god of the covenant and of loyalty, who presided over the judgment of souls. Mehr's Western dates are September 23 to October 22; its astrological sign is Libra, the scales.

**ABAN**. The eighth month's name commemorates another Zoroastrian water deity. Its Western dates are October 23 to November 21; its astrological sign is Scorpio, the scorpion.

**AZAR**. This month bears the name of a Zoroastrian fire god. Its Western dates are November 22 to December 21; its astrological sign is Sagittarius, the archer.

**DEY**. The tenth month's name means "creator," and the whole period once was dedicated to the Lord of Wisdom, Ahura Mazda. It used to begin with a feast of charity, when people devoted themselves to helping others. Dey's Western dates are December 22 to January 20; its astrological sign is Capricorn, the goat.

**BAHMAN**. This month echoes the name of a deity that meant "good purpose." He was a protector of animals, and more than that, a symbol of creative goodness and cosmic order. Bahman's Western dates are January 21 to February 19; its astrological sign is Aquarius, the water bearer.

**ESFAND**. The last month of the Iranian year is called after the venerable earth mother – counterpart of the Greek Demeter – whose name meant "holy devotion," and who guarded herdsmen and farmers. Esfand's Western dates are February 20 to March 20; its astrological sign is Pisces, the fish.

# A Legacy of the Chinese Zodiac

**The Mongols invaded Iran** in the thirteenth century and left devastation in their wake. Yet these invaders also introduced a kind of calendar so appealing that Persians use it to this day. This is the twelve-year cycle of the Chinese zodiac.

China has dozens of legends about the arrangement of the years. A popular tale says that the Jade Emperor, lord of the heavens, commanded thirteen animals to race across a river, the hierarchy to be determined by their order of arrival. Among them was a cat, which was reluctant to swim. The clever rat suggested they both ride across on the back of the ox. They did. As they neared the finish, however, the rat pushed the cat into the water and jumped ashore, thereby winning first place and ensuring eternal enmity between cats – who lost their chance to name a year – and rats.

In the Chinese cycle of years, as shown in the illustration on pages 114–15, the animals are particularly important because they help determine the character of a year – and of all the people born in that year.

**A RAT YEAR** is one of plenty and good prospects.

**AN OX YEAR** is one of diligent work and domestic trials.

**A TIGER YEAR** is one of ferocity and wars.

**A RABBIT YEAR** is placid and congenial.

**A DRAGON  YEAR** is filled with ambition and daring.

**A SNAKE YEAR** is quiet on the surface but unpredictable.

**A HORSE YEAR** is lively and adventurous.

**A GOAT YEAR** is tranquil and creative.

**A MONKEY YEAR** is exciting and full of invention.

**A ROOSTER YEAR** is uneasily balanced and often conflict-filled.

**A DOG YEAR** offers harmony at home and rebellions abroad.

**A PIG YEAR** brings each cycle to a close with prosperity and contentment.

# The Animal Cycle of Years

**DRAGONS** are wealthy, wise, and powerful; eccentric, honest, and brave. Their friends are the Rat and the Monkey, but not the Dog. Dragons are born in the years 1928, 1940, 1952, 1964, 1976, 1988, 2000.

**SNAKES** are quiet, deep, and wise; determined, vain, and intense. Their friends are the Ox and the Rooster, but not the Pig. Snakes are born in the years 1929, 1941, 1953, 1965, 1977, 1989, 2001.

**HORSES** are popular and cheerful; independent, quick, and artful. Their friends are the Tiger and the Dog, but not the Rat. Horses are born in the years 1930, 1942, 1954, 1966, 1978, 1990, 2002.

**GOATS** are religious, creative, and shy; elegant, emphatic, and wise. Their friends are the Rabbit and the Pig, but not the Ox. Goats are born in the years 1931, 1943, 1955, 1967, 1979, 1991, 2003.

**MONKEYS** are smart, skillful, and successful; they are knowledgeable and discriminating. Their friends are the Dragon and the Rat, but not the Tiger. Monkeys are born in the years 1932, 1944, 1956, 1968, 1980, 1992, 2004.

**ROOSTERS** are ambitious, hard-working, and adventurous; deep-thinking, eccentric, and opinionated. Their friends are the Snake and the Ox, but not the Rabbit. Roosters are born in the years 1933, 1945, 1957, 1969, 1981, 1993, 2005.

**RABBITS** are lucky, virtuous, and reserved; talented, affectionate, and long-lived. Their friends are the Goat and the Pig, but not the Rooster. Rabbits are born in the years 1927, 1939, 1951, 1963, 1975, 1987, 1999.

**TIGERS** are powerful, protective, and sympathetic; short-tempered, deep-thinking, and courageous. Their friends are the Horse and the Dog, but not the Monkey. Tigers are born in the years 1926, 1938, 1950, 1962, 1974, 1986, 1998.

**OXEN** are patient, confident, and eccentric; quiet, strong, and stubborn. Their friends are the Snake and the Rooster, but not the Goat. Oxen are born in the years 1937, 1949, 1961, 1973, 1985, 1997, 2009.

**RATS ARE** charming, picky, and thrifty; ambitious, adventurous, and deep-thinking. Their friends are the Dragon and the Monkey, but not the Horse. Rats are born in the years 1936, 1948, 1960, 1972, 1984, 1996, 2008.

**PIGS ARE** ambitious, strong, and honest; wealthy, studious, and kind. Their friends are the Rabbit and the Goat, but not the Snake. Pigs are born in the years 1935, 1947, 1959, 1971, 1983, 1995, 2007.

**DOGS ARE** loyal, honest, and cooperative; faithful, confident, and eccentric. Their friends are the Tiger and the Horse, but not the Dragon. Dogs are born in the years 1934, 1946, 1958, 1970, 1982, 1994, 2006.

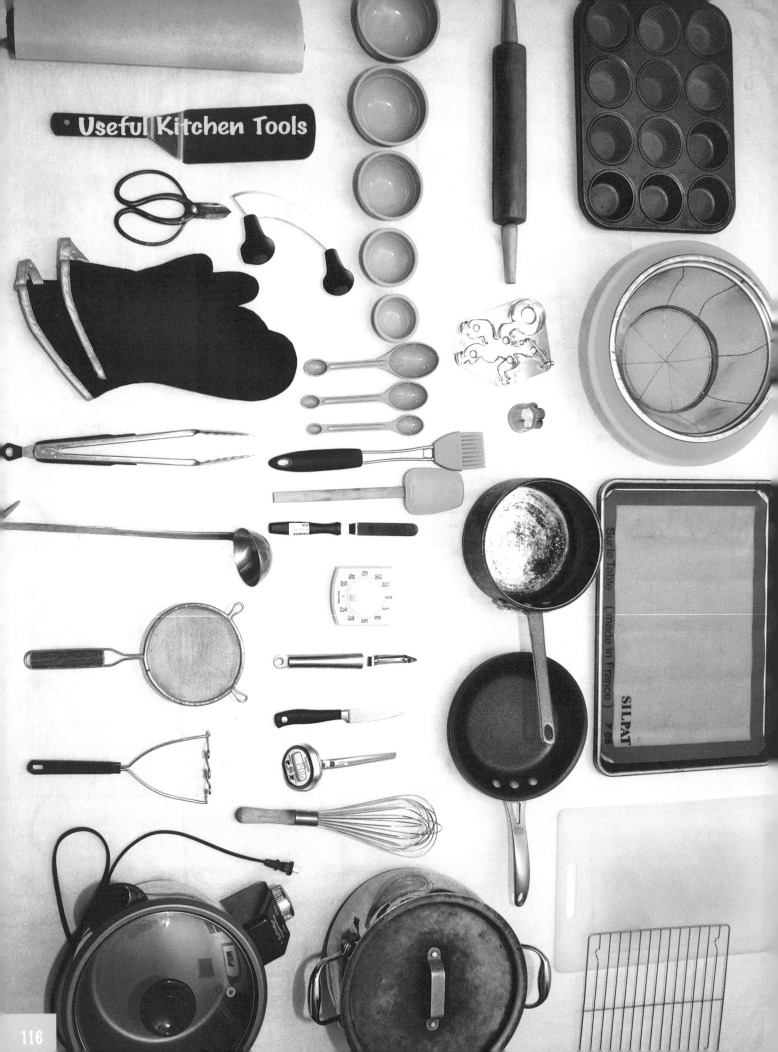

Useful Kitchen Tools

# Haji Firuz Cookie Cutter Template

If you do not have the stainless steel Haji Firuz cookie cutter, use tracing paper to transfer this template onto a piece of cardboard, and cut around it using scissors. Use the cardboard template to cutout the dough in the Haji Firuz Gingerbread Cookies recipe on page 75 by placing it onto your dough and cutting around it with a sharp knife.

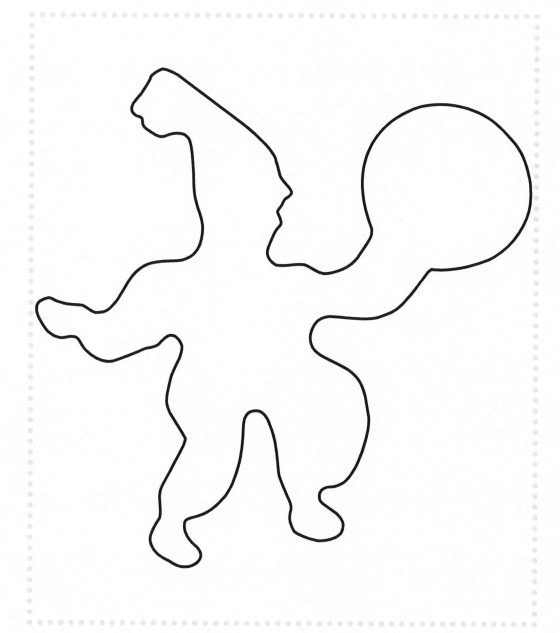

# Credits & Acknowledgments

All photos by Chris Eichler, copyright © 2006–7 Mage Publishers, except as listed below.

Images and photos courtesy of:

Haji Firuz paintings on the cover and endpapers and on pages 14, 15, and 17,
  details, Haji Firuz © Ardeshir Mohassess.

Pages 18, Goldfish, 19 Carpet Washing photos © Fataneh Dadkhah.

Page 16, Entertainers, circa 1600, painting by Mirza Mohammad al-Hoseyni, photo © Freer Gallery of Art,
  Smithsonian Institution.

Pages: 10 and 118, Parade of Nations Carving, Apadana Palace Staircase (rh357–1666 and 1672),
  photos © David Poole/Robert Harding World Imagery/Getty Images.

Pages 42 and 53, painting by Mohammad Siah Qalam (Mohammad Naqqash), late fifteenth century, H2160,
  folio, 77b, photo © Topkapi Palace Museum.

Page 43, Reza Abassi, Youth Reading, circa 1625–6, British Museum, London, 1920-9-17-0298.

Page 44, Detail of a Relief of a Lion Attacking a Bull on the Tripylon Stairway in Persepolis, Iran © Corbis.

Page 52, painting of outdoor picnic, sixteenth century, British Library, London.

Pages 5, 20, 21, 95, 105-107 photos © M. Batmanglij.

Page 15 translation of Haji Firuz song, Dick Davis.

I would like to thank Ellen Phillips, who helped me greatly with the writing and editing of the first draft of the text.

I am most thankful to the wonderful children whose pictures appear in these pages – all of whom I have known and loved since they were born: Olivia, Hugh, Penelope, Cyrus, Sabrina, Sanam, Kurosh, and Tina. They were wonderful, and working with them was truly enjoyable. Thanks are also due to their parents, who were most helpful and positive about this project at a very busy time in their lives.

My special thanks to my own children (not children anymore, of course), Zal and Rostam, for their avant-garde comments and sense of design, and their encouragement. Creating this book allows us to share with other children what they experienced during their childhood. I would also like to thank their aunts, *Khaleh* Faezeh and *Ameh* Shahla, for all their help.

I am grateful to my cousin, Hossein, whose cream puff recipe I have adapted here. I also had a great deal of assistance from my interns during this project and want to thank them all for everything they did to help: Nelly Lewis at the start, Lily Warner, Joshua Henderson, Greg Deorio, and Jonathan Momolo.

Finally, many thanks to Chris Eichler who took most of the photographs for this book.

CPSIA information can be obtained
at www.ICGtesting.com
Printed in the USA
LVHW070725140419
614066LV00002BA/2/P